WELFARE, POPULISM
AND WELFARE CHAUVINISM

Also available in the series

Dualisation of part-time work
The development of labour market insiders and outsiders

Edited by **Heidi Nicolaisen, Hanne Kavli and Ragnhild Steen Jensen**

This book brings together leading international authors from a number of fields to provide an up to date understanding of part-time work at national, sector, industry and workplace levels.

HB £75.00 **ISBN** 978-1-4473-4860-3
248 pages June 2019

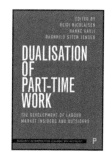

Forthcoming titles

The moral economy of activation
Ideas, politics and policies

By **Magnus Hansen**

By rethinking the role of ideas and morality in policy changes, this book illustrates how the moral economy of activation leads to a permanent behaviourist testing of the unemployed in public debate as well as in local jobcentres.

HB £75.00 **ISBN** 978-1-4473-4996-9
208 pages September 2019

Local policies and the European Social Fund
Employment policies across Europe

By **Katharina Zimmermann**

Comparing data from 18 local case studies across 6 European countries, and deploying an innovative mixed-method approach, this book presents comparative evidence on everyday challenges in the context of the European Social Fund (ESF) and discusses how these findings are applicable to other funding schemes.

HB £75.00 **ISBN** 978-1-4473-4651-7
224 pages October 2019

For a full list of all titles in the series visit:

**www.bristoluniversitypress.co.uk/
research-in-comparative-and-global-social-policy-1**

WELFARE, POPULISM AND WELFARE CHAUVINISM

Bent Greve

First published in Great Britain in 2019 by

Policy Press
University of Bristol
1-9 Old Park Hill
Bristol
BS2 8BB
UK
t: +44 (0)117 954 5940
pp-info@bristol.ac.uk
www.policypress.co.uk

North America office:
Policy Press
c/o The University of Chicago Press
1427 East 60th Street
Chicago, IL 60637, USA
t: +1 773 702 7700
f: +1 773-702-9756
sales@press.uchicago.edu
www.press.uchicago.edu

British Library Cataloguing in Publication Data
A catalogue record for this book is available from the British Library

Library of Congress Cataloging-in-Publication Data
A catalog record for this book has been requested

978-1-4473-5043-9 hardback
978-1-4473-5046-0 ePdf
978-1-4473-5050-7 ePub
978-1-4473-5051-4 Mobi

Cover design by Andrew Corbett
Printed and bound in Great Britain by CPI Group (UK) Ltd, Croydon, CR0 4YY
Policy Press uses environmentally responsible print partners

Contents

List of tables and figures

Tables

Figures

Series preface

Heejung Chung (University of Kent, UK)
Alexandra Kaasch (University of Bielefeld, Germany)
Stefan Kühner (Lingnan University, Hong Kong)

In a world that is rapidly changing, increasingly connected and uncertain, there is a need to develop a shared applied policy analysis of welfare regimes around the globe. *Research in Comparative and Global Social Policy* is a series of books that addresses broad questions around how nation states and transnational policy actors manage globally shared challenges. In so doing, the book series includes a wide array of contributions, which discuss comparative social policy history, development and reform within a broad international context. Initially conceived during a meeting of the UK Social Policy Association Executive Committee in 2016, the book series invites innovative research by leading experts on all world regions and global social policy actors and aims to fulfil the following objectives: it encourages cross-disciplinary approaches that develop theoretical frameworks reaching across individual world regions and global actors; it seeks to provide evidence-based good practice examples that cross the bridge between academic research and practice; not least, it aims to provide a platform in which a wide range of innovative methodological approaches, may it be national case studies, larger-N comparative studies, or global social policy studies can be introduced to aid the evaluation, design, and implementation of future social policies.

This monograph by Bent Greve tackles one of the most poignant challenges faced by many welfare states – the issue of rising anti-immigrant attitudes and, with it, populist parties. In this book, Greve asks the important question: why is it, in these times of growing inequality and polarisation of life chances across the population, that citizens are using their democratic power to vote for parties that reduce welfare and put themselves at greater risk? The book brings together a wide range of theoretical concepts drawn from the welfare attitudes and welfare state legitimacy literature, alongside a range of recent quantitative and qualitative data, to answer this question in greater depth. The main argument is that the rise in inequality and dualisation of the labour market observed across Europe has led to diminished trust not only between citizens and the state, but also amongst the population – an increase in attitudes of 'us vs. them'.

This growing distrust, Greve goes on to explain, is linked with rising welfare chauvinism and the stigmatisation of benefit claimants, which, in turn, is related to the rise of populist right-wing parties and may end up benefitting the rich, and dividing societies even further. By making these crucial links, this book provides readers with important perspectives on how to understand the increasing political turmoil we face across the world and shows possible ways forward in the future. As the first book of our series, it sets the scene for other books to follow by tackling large global questions with innovative and rigorous analysis to help both academics and policy makers to understand the issues better and find appropriate solutions.

Preface

A growing economic divide has been witnessed in many countries. There also seems to have been an increase in the social divide, and increasing numbers of people becoming discontent with the development in their country, their own standard of living and economic options. The divide is often between different geographic areas and specific sectors in various countries. Part of this reflects a classical and ongoing transformation of labour markets in all countries, and with all kinds of change, there will be winners and losers.

This time, the changes might be stronger than in previous times as a consequence of new technology, as well as of growing international migration and, in certain years, refugees fleeing civil war wanting, especially, to enter Europe. Both these issues have put pressure on welfare states and their development, in addition to the pressure caused by demographic transitions.

At the same time, this seems to have had an impact on voters' behaviour in such a way that we have seen an increase in support for more populist parties around Europe and a president in the US with a stronger focus on the US than global development. We have witnessed a referendum in the UK as a result of which the UK will leave the European Union (EU), now known as Brexit. We have seen stronger national statements from people and parties around Europe, and we have witnessed stronger viewpoints on the positions of migrants and/or refugees.

There has been a growing discussion on welfare chauvinism, but also on austerity and the reduction of the role of the welfare state, at least in some countries. Based on this, the inspiration for this book comes from a profound interest in trying to understand why and how these trends could have and have had an impact on welfare state development. This also includes why people are in favour of, and/or against, specific changes to the welfare state. Historically, the legitimacy of at least part of the welfare state has been on the agenda for a long time, but it now seems to be increasing in importance more than ever.

I hope that this book can contribute to the understanding of the continued role of the welfare state in times of change. It does this by the interpretation of existing data in a new way and the inclusion of new data released by the European Social Survey in late 2017, updated in May 2018, on the legitimacy of the welfare state.

The breakdown of the book is such that I have written Chapters 1 to 6 and Chapter 9, with Chapters 7 and 8 co-authored with my colleague Anders Ejrnæs.

Thanks to my research group at Roskilde University for constructive and critical comments on the outline of the book, and discussions along the way. Thanks also for comments from reviewers on the outline and the first draft of the book.

Bagsværd and Roskilde, November 2018

What is it all about?

Introduction

We have seen tendencies towards stronger support for what are labelled populist parties in many countries; support for right-wing parties often with an agenda of reducing taxes – and thus implicitly welfare state retrenchment in the years to come – but also for right-wing parties with a negative stance towards migrants and a focus on support for welfare to the deserving native population. The UK has decided to leave the European Union (EU) due to, among other things, a negative perception of the free movement of workers within the EU, but also because at least some voters perceive that decisions were taken at too far a distance from them. The blaming of the EU and a more national stance has been witnessed in several other European countries. In the US, the election of Trump as president, also with a rhetoric of them and us, can be seen in this light. He even 'garnered votes from immigrants, Muslims and other minorities, women, and unionized workers, in spite of the fact that in previous months he had behaved or advocated policies against their interest' (Wilkinson and Klaes, 2018: 3). There has been an argument for retrenchment in many countries in the wake of the financial crisis in order to cope with high public-sector deficits as a consequence of both supporting the financial sector and the increased pressure on societies as a consequence of the fiscal crisis. Austerity measures have been seen as important to cope with the rules within the euro area, although, as the book shows, it is not so simple to find austerity in all countries and all areas of welfare state development. These attitudes and votes go against the rational behaviour of individuals used in economic textbooks, and thus call for an analysis including an interdisciplinary approach from sociology, political science, psychology and behavioural economics.

We have witnessed stronger and more dual labour markets, and options and possibilities that societies will become even more segregated (Greve, 2017). There are varieties of gated communities that have developed not only in the US (Putnam, 2015), but also in Europe. Why is it that despite the fact that, in many ways, there is a need for more welfare, also as an investment into societies' development, the trend seems to be moving in the other direction, with the discrediting of the welfare state's ability both to deliver welfare services and to support people in need thereof? Lastly, why not help in redistributing consumption possibilities over the life course (Yerkes and Peper, 2019), and why neglect to look at public spending as an important social investment (Morel et al, 2012)? The fact is that many voters and people still seemingly question the role of at least part of the welfare state, and support retrenchment. They do not, perhaps, support retrenchment per se, but their voting behaviour might have this consequence. This is not to venture into debates of false consciousness, as in the 1970s, but more a reflection upon the fact that, for a variety of reasons, something has presumably not worked well in modern welfare states.

As a consequence of the developments on the labour market, as well as other policies in welfare states, we have witnessed an increase in inequalities in many countries (Piketty, 2014; OECD, 2017). This has happened despite the fact that there is increasing knowledge about the possible negative impact on societies' development, including on economic growth, of high levels of economic inequality. In recent years, this has also caught the interest of international organisations such as the Organisation for Economic Co-operation and Development (OECD), the EU and the International Monetary Fund (IMF) (Cingano, 2014, Dabla-Norris et al, 2015, Eurostat, 2017), and it was also on the agenda at the World Economic Forum in Davos in January 2018. An increase in inequality might also negatively influence health (Pickett and Wilkinson, 2009, 2018).

The negative perception of, for example, the free movement of workers is often held without even having a strong factual knowledge of the actual size of the benefit or the economic consequences. Although knowledge about the overall impact of migration and refugees might also be limited, stories about the impact on, or a feeling that this has implications for, individuals' opportunities and living standards at the micro-level can be part of the picture.

Therefore, the puzzle is voters' behaviour, such as voting for parties with an agenda of welfare chauvinism that might imply less welfare state, which conflicts with what they actually need in order to have a high quality of life. Therefore, in principle, it could be more in their interest to pursue other approaches. In many countries, right-wing parties have gained an increased number of votes, from an average of less than 10% in Europe in 1985 to 18.5% in 2017[1]. There is variation across countries, and in some, there has also been support for left-wing populist parties. Naturally, in all countries, despite the growth in support for parties with a strong negative view on migrants, they have gained formal power only to a more limited extent, such as in France, the UK, Germany and Sweden, albeit that gaining formal power has been the case in, for example, Hungary, Austria, Greece and Italy. However, even in countries without formal power, they have influenced the ideas of policymakers by presenting their viewpoints – and ideas, as covered in more detail in Chapter 2, can have an influence on social policy (Béland, 2005, 2018). This is because populist parties have influenced governments even in countries where they have no formal power. In a way, this reflects the old debate on the median voter's impact on growth in public sector spending (Downs, 1957; Doel and Velthoven, 1993), although here with a more negative result for welfare states, or at least part of welfare states (see more in Chapter 5). Furthermore, this is despite the impact of the median voter being dependent on whether preferences overlap between policy areas. However, some populist parties have, by now, developed viewpoints that to a larger degree seem to include at the very least positive aspects related to those who they find are deserving of welfare support, such as the elderly, although they do not always push these viewpoints. A classical social policy discussion of the deserving and undeserving is thereby increasing in importance. This is also influencing the conditionality of benefits (Watts and Fitzpatrick, 2018). The understanding of deservingness by trying to attach stigma also has an impact (Baumberger, 2016).

Often, global economic development is embraced by those referred to as the elite, whereas those at risk of losing their jobs or status are more reluctant to support, and might even be directly against, such development. The ability of countries to pursue their own policies can have an impact on voters' negative perception of what might, in fact, be a positive development; in Europe, this could be a reason why voters might be reluctant to support the EU and be against more decisions taken at the European level as they might even believe that national decisions are better due to the promise from populist parties, as in the Brexit debate. The election of Trump also points towards what populism is about: the people versus the elite (discussed in Chapter 2).

Growing economic inequality (see more in Chapter 4) has, without doubt, had an impact on the development and how the situation is witnessed by different groups. It has caused a stronger divide in societies, and this divide has presumably fed back into the understanding of how societies should and can develop. The same can be expected due to the increase in inequality and the rapid change in labour markets, making it more difficult for many to get an income above the poverty level, get a decent job and have the expectation that their children can have a better life than themselves. Therefore, there is good reason to expect that overall changes in welfare spending and inequality (including the working poor), and growing difficulties for low-income and even middle-income groups to get a strong position in the labour market, influence the development and possible support for populist parties. Therefore, these three elements are described and analysed in detail, including developments in recent years, in order to form a background for understanding the context of change in the perception of, legitimacy of and support for the welfare state (see more in Chapters 3 to 5).

In general, European people support the welfare state: most believe that goals related to poverty and inequality are achieved, and 'more than half believe that policy outcomes such as benefit levels and the quality of services are insufficient' (Roosma et al, 2013: 243). However, there are also around 40% who find that the welfare state harms the economy (this is based upon data from 2008, ie, before the financial crisis). Thus, this might also have an impact on support for the welfare state and populist viewpoints on the role of the state.

Overall, the book tries to disentangle the contrasting viewpoints on welfare state development arising from the views of the population and populist parties, including those views on central issues such as migrants and refugees – the conflict between supporting those in need of support from the welfare state (due to changes in the labour market, growing inequalities, etc) and how and why voters support political developments that, if looked at from the perspective of what could help improve their daily life and quality of life in the longer term, do the opposite. It is also an attempt to analyse and understand the ongoing change in a variety of different welfare states that can, in the long run, have strong implications for the survival of the idea of a welfare state as a collective good. Naturally, the situation is different in various countries as a consequence of historical legacies and economic/political contexts, but there is still a need to try to understand what is actually going on.

Key points and questions for the book to delve into are:

1. Will populists erode or support welfare state development?
2. Can a populist and chauvinist stance explain specific traits in welfare state development?
3. Is it possible that populist development will imply the restructuring of the welfare state, especially if there is decreased trust in welfare state administration and politicians?

What should be analysed?

Following the points mentioned earlier, there are several interrelated issues to be analysed. One is whether there has, in fact, been the retrenchment of welfare states, and, if so, whether this has been in areas that can be seen as important from a populist and welfare chauvinist perspective, or whether this is a more general trend in line with neoliberal thinking about societies' development, such as austerity as the only game in town (Piketty, 2014, 2016; Mason, 2016; Klein, 2017; Taylor-Gooby et al, 2017; Varoufakis, 2017). In Chapter 5, this book gives input to answer the question of populist impact in recent years on welfare states overall and development in specific parts of the welfare states. The book also probes into whether, and to what degree, there have been developments towards a larger degree of inequality. Thus, it also tries to find out whether, for example, changes in the social security and tax system, with lower taxes on high-income earners – despite no clear knowledge on the possible impact of changes in the tax system on overall economic development – have taken place, and how they have influenced the level of equality. This increase in inequality, besides negative effects on issues such as health (Wilkinson and Pickett, 2018), might also give rise to a stronger feeling of them and us (see Chapter 6).

The focus on, and relationship between, welfare chauvinism and populism is due to the fact that these approaches seem to focus on positions influencing not only legitimacy, but also the welfare state itself, and is thus an optimal issue to examine in order to grasp the contradictory viewpoints of voters and thereby the developments in different countries. The legitimacy of welfare states has been questioned from the perspectives of both efficiency and whether the goals of justice, redistribution and support for economic development have been achieved. So, here, the possible dilemma revolves around the fact that even if something has been delivered, it has not lived up to expectations, at least not to the extent expected by citizens, implying that some of them have looked for different scapegoats – these being the elite, individual migrants or the grand narrative of the positive impact of globalisation – towards whom they can direct their aggression and frustration (Romano, 2018). The fact that globalisation and free trade can be shown to improve overall economic options at the macro-level does not imply that this is felt at the micro-level when a workplace is closed down due to outsourcing (Autor et al, 2016). Many populist parties in Europe have a right-wing approach, combining nationalism with a negative stance towards migrants.

However, both in Europe and around the world, such as in Greece and South-America, there is also left-wing populism, meaning that populism is not only a right-wing issue. This is reflected in the analysis.

One hypothesis to investigate further in the analysis is whether it can be shown that the development has been positive, in particular, for social benefits and services that, at least until now, can be seen as, and are expected to be, directed mainly towards natives, that is, following a welfare chauvinism approach. This would point to the fact that benefits and services in relation to health care and old age have been at least stable or even increasing, whereas it is the opposite in relation to unemployment benefit/social assistance, and perhaps also child benefits, as in the wake of the increased free movement of workers, there has been pressure to ensure that people residing in a country for a short while are only entitled to limited access to these benefits (Oorschot and Roosma, 2015).

The analysis is carried out not only by looking into perceptions, although this is important, but also by probing into the actual development before and after the crisis in core sectors of welfare states. Given the possible impact of the financial crisis on welfare states, welfare attitudes data are also taken from before and after the crisis. Naturally, the analytical points described need to be seen in the light of the aspects covered earlier.

Some methodological considerations

The book is a combination of desktop research based upon already-existing research in the field, especially including detailed qualitative studies from, in particular, the US and the UK (Putnam, 2015; Hochschild, 2016; Winlow et al, 2017). These different studies frame the background for the discussion on the deeper understanding of why, despite the fact that they could gain from increased state spending on welfare, people perhaps choose other pathways when they vote. This also points to the fact that there are shortcomings in quantitative data on attitudes (Oorschot and Roosma, 2015; Chung et al, 2018).

The desktop study is combined with more quantitative-based analysis using Eurostat and OECD data as these are central to depicting changes in welfare state spending and generosity, and several waves of the European Social Survey (ESS) are utilised. These data have made it possible to be relatively up to date both on viewpoints related to trust and legitimacy in welfare states, and also on the development over time – thus also making it possible to tap into the impact of the latest financial crisis on viewpoints on central and important aspects of welfare state development. Trust has been a recurring theme in the ESS. Welfare attitudes were a specific rotating module in round 4 of the ESS (in 2008). This is combined with data from round 8 of the ESS (in 2016) (which also had a special module on welfare attitudes). This can be used as this information provides options for looking into the situation before and after the financial crisis on core aspects such as government responsibilities and satisfaction with welfare state performance. The fourth round found a clear east–west divide (European Social Survey, 2012), and an issue to look into[2] is whether this divide on attitudes in relation to welfare states still exists. Lastly, data on public opinion in the EU are utilised, from which it is possible to obtain information on what concerns people in the EU in their own countries, both before the financial crisis and change thereafter, as part of the explanation for welfare state development in Europe (European Commission, 2018).

The book further condenses many of the existing articles within the field to depict whether there are some common trends or issues that one can use in order to provide an answer to the possible contradictions presented earlier. The book tries, in a classical way, to see whether different types of welfare states have had the same development, given that context matters. However, instead of using the traditional three worlds of welfare capitalism (Esping-Andersen, 1990), it includes countries in Europe – north, south, east and west – as there seems to be a strong division within Europe along these axes. Reference to the US is also provided as there are qualitative studies on the development in the US, and as there seem to be differences in the populations' viewpoints on equality (Alesina et al, 2004). In some instances, the book covers more EU countries in order to depict the changes to a greater extent within welfare state development in Europe. Thus, in general, countries that are included in the presentation, at a minimum, are: Denmark and Sweden (Nordic); the UK and Ireland (liberal, west); Germany and France (Continental, west); Italy and Spain (south); and Poland and the Czech Republic (east). However, the quantitative comparison of the development from 2008 to 2016 from ESS survey data is restricted by the countries that participated in both years (see more in Chapter 7).

The time frame used is dependent on data availability, so information before and after the financial crisis is included as far as possible. This is not only because the financial crisis has had a direct impact on economies, spending on welfare and increases in unemployment, but also because it seems to have influenced the level of well-being and happiness in many countries. A declining level of life satisfaction might

7

also be an issue influencing how voters see and prefer to have the development.

Overall, the book thus combines quantitative data with existing qualitative informed analysis on welfare state development, and through the use of existing knowledge, tries further to make a synthesis of the existing studies. In this way, several perspectives can be triangulated to present a coherent picture of why we have seen these contradictions in the perception of, and development in, welfare states, especially in Europe. This approach is also chosen as a consequence of the limitations of the quantitative analysis of welfare state developments, which risks not including central details, institutional change and context for the analysis of the development (Spicker, 2018).

A short overview of the chapters

Overall, the book is split into several parts. The first two chapters set the scene and explain the core concepts that are analysed in the book. Chapters 3 to 5 depict possible core issues of the development influencing the perception of welfare states (spending, inequality and labour market development). The analysis in Chapters 6 and 7 is based upon different types of available data related to issues such as welfare state attitudes, welfare chauvinism and indications of why populism is possible, such as related to trust in government. Chapter 8 focuses on populism and viewpoints related to migrants, and Chapter 9 sums up the analysis and presents possible conclusions.

Thus, after this first chapter, Chapter 2 presents some of the basic concepts that are used throughout the book as analysis and debate on welfare state developments often use these concepts, albeit without a clear presentation of how they can actually be understood, and how this might influence development. Voters' and citizens' perception of what would be the best way for a welfare state to develop are thus often analysed using an assortment of concepts, a variety of theoretical angles and different perspectives. The basic concepts to be included are: welfare chauvinism, legitimacy, deserving/undeserving, populism and ideas. They are presented, albeit briefly, as this helps to frame the presentation of the content of the book, and also because several of these concepts are not always used consistently and/or do not have connotations that implicitly indicate a normative position by the user. Still, these concepts are influential – some have been for many years – in the understanding of why welfare states have developed as they have. Within the area of legitimacy, issues related to trust in decision-makers are also included because, in some countries, trust in welfare states can have an impact on the possible support for the continued development of the welfare state.

As argued earlier, we have seen an increase in inequality. Chapter 3 focuses on why inequality matters. It does this by systematising the knowledge that we have on why inequality matters – for economic growth, for health and for social cohesion – and why trickle-down economics does not work. This is done, first, by showing the development using traditional aspects such as the Gini coefficient, but also by reflecting and showing data for inequality in health and how this can be seen as connected to changes in economic inequality. Real-wage development is also included as a reason why there has been increasing inequality, combined with inequality in wealth and capital income. So, even if people get a job (as is part of the focus of Chapter 7), this is not a guarantee that they will have a standard of living above the poverty line, being, in fact, the working poor. Inequality is not only an issue related to the economic sphere of societal development; therefore, the chapter also points towards other types of inequality.

Another central issue having an impact on, and seemingly moving countries towards, increasingly split societies is covered in Chapter 4: the dualisation of the labour market, or, more simply, the need for jobs for persons with different qualifications, including fewer jobs for low-skilled persons. The increased divide in the labour market, connected to the ability to be included in or excluded from society and to access different goods and services, might be an explanation as to why populist parties have been able to get support as they reflect upon and argue that they can do something in relation to these issues. Therefore, the chapter depicts, in some detail, the consequences for social cohesion resulting from recent labour market developments. It includes a short description of possible future trends in the labour market and how this can influence the development of welfare states. It further includes reference to the globalisation discussion as this is also an issue in relation to labour market developments.

There have been discussions on austerity and reduction in welfare states, and in order to depict whether this is actually the case, Chapter 5 presents a few facts on spending on welfare states. The chapter thus shows the development in spending on welfare states from before to after the financial crisis, and splits the development into areas often having high legitimacy, as argued earlier (old age and health), versus areas having a low level of support (income benefits to the unemployed and migrants). The issue is whether we have or have not seen retrenchment in general or in specific areas, supporting a hypothesis about support from voters for delivering welfare mainly to areas/persons seen as deserving (often being national citizens), in line with a welfare chauvinism agenda. This is also connected to the debates on the fact that we adapt, so that it might be that even a standstill in spending is felt as retrenchment because we have got used to it, and if someone else gets something, we might feel this as a loss (Kahneman, 2011).

After this more quantitative-oriented chapter, Chapter 6 looks into stories about people's perception of welfare state developments and why they do not trust the political system and the administration, or what is often labelled the elite. The chapter draws on a number of recent books and articles trying to depict and understand people's opinion – from Brexit to the vote for Trump – where one might witness a contradiction between possible self-interest and support for populist viewpoints (eg Putnam, 2015; Hochschild, 2016; Vance, 2016; Winlow et al, 2017). The attempt here is also to systematise why, especially, low-income groups with a precarious position in the labour market (if they have a job at all) vote for populist and/or liberal policies that might not improve their standard of living at the end of day. The possible distance between 'them and us' as a theme is also included. It also refers back to the populist understanding that they represent the 'people', whereas the elite are ruling against the interests of the people. In a way, this also reflects the historical understanding that there is a 'silent majority' that the populists represent, who, due to the elite, have not had the option to be present in policy decisions. People seem to have a need to belong to, and be part of, a group, and this can naturally influence their perception of how society should develop.

A central question is whether it is possible to depict and understand when and how there have been changes in citizens' perception of, and trust in, societies' development, which is the focus of Chapter 7. Using data from the ESS, European public opinion, Eurostat and other quantitative information, the intention is to look into the development in attitudes related to:

- who should have the responsibility for providing welfare;
- how the trust in central institutions in welfare states has developed; and
- the balance between these issues and what the consequences of the actual development have been, as depicted in Chapter 5.

Chapter 8 looks specifically into the possible relation between immigrants, populism and welfare chauvinism by depicting, first, the rise in populism, as also touched upon in Chapters 1 and 2, and then attitudes towards migrants related to questions such as whether they get more than they contribute, positions related to a multicultural society and whether to allow more or fewer migrants.

Lastly, the concluding Chapter 9 focuses on how to interpret the position of, and attitudes towards, welfare states, while, at the same time, pointing to what can be done to improve and develop welfare states in such a way that they will benefit a greater group of people and ensure coherent and stable societies.

Delimitations

As always, a book cannot go into depth in all detail and include all possible terrains to explain the development. Thus, more specific policy analysis of individual countries' policies is mainly left out, as well as analysis of different political parties' percentage of votes or members or seats in parliament, although, some reflections are made on the impact of political parties in passing.[3] This also reflects the fact that it might not always be the size of the party that can influence the development, but rather the ability to be an agenda-setter. How actual change in policy influences public opinion, a kind of reverse causality, is outside the scope of this book (however, for an example from Sweden, see Bendz, 2017).

Globalisation's and new technology's impact on jobs are part of the new types of risk influencing people's everyday life, which thereby have an impact on how individuals perceive the welfare state. The economic and political pressures on welfare states have had a possible impact, not only as a consequence of globalisation, but also due to demographic changes, international migration and, in several countries, continuously high levels of unemployment, especially in the wake of the last financial crisis. Globalisation as such is not included, but it can be seen more as a background variable that, in combination with technological changes, influences the availability of jobs for some, which is part of Chapter 7. Europeanisation, per se, including the issue of a social Europe (Baute et al, 2018), is not included in the chapter; however, it does include the perception and discussion of the free movement of workers within the EU and how this has influenced the options of workers in several countries and, relatedly, the options for getting a job. Deservingness is also influenced by the size of free movement and migration (increase or decrease). Globalisation is touched upon briefly, particularly as regards the possible impact on labour market development. Media coverage has an impact on how citizens and voters perceive the actual and expected future situation.

As this is not a part of this book, for an example of such an analysis, see instead Esmark and Schoop (2017).

The debate on the impact of the neoliberal agenda is not included, neither is the, by now, rather old discussion on the competition state (Cerny, 1997) and how these ideas have been used as an argument for necessary changes in societies' development. Again, as with globalisation, this is an issue in the background, framing and influencing some of the ideas and questions regarding welfare state development. However, the book does not need to go into whether the competition state in itself is a reason for welfare chauvinism and populism as it is more the concrete change in welfare states that might be important to investigate, which is depicted in Chapter 5.

Whether and how the bribing of the middle class has been part of welfare state development, and the fact that changes in welfare states and the position of the middle class have influenced the development, are only part of the presentation to a more limited extent. The same relates to possible discussion on whether the changes influence the so-called generational contract, for example, where one generation pays for welfare with the expectation that the next generation will pay for their welfare, although the ageing population can influence this (Birnbaum et al, 2017). The historical reasons for not developing perhaps more universal welfare states are not part of the analysis. An example of this is that the ethno-national diversity of the US might have been a hindrance for a generous welfare state, and still today 'white voters in the South are sceptical of a welfare state that promises to deliver generous support to black Americans in northern cities, or to Latin Americans in California' (Avent, 2017: 225). This reflects an early type of welfare chauvinism.

The possible impact of populism dependent on the national electoral system is outside the scope of the book. It will presumably depend on the electoral system as countries with first-past-the-post systems, and thereby often with fewer political parties, might be less directly influenced, although political pressure for change can be witnessed even in these countries, see, for example, the decision on Brexit in the UK. The median voter's possible influence is, however, touched upon.

Moral psychology is outside the scope of the book, despite the fact that it might help in the understanding of citizens' perception of what to do and how this can influence who they vote for (see, instead, Haidt, 2013). A few examples of viewpoints are, however, included in Chapter 6. Welfare state development is also influenced by occupational welfare, but this has been left outside the scope of, and in relation to, welfare chauvinism, despite the argument that occupational welfare is especially available for those who have actually been in the labour market (but see the special issue of *Social Policy & Administration* [2018], vol 52, no 2).

Conclusion

The scene is now set for what the book analyses and how it does so. Thus, the core issues are central aspects related to welfare state development in different countries and frames that might help in explaining why this has happened, including support for welfare states. How and why have we seen a development with approaches in a welfare chauvinist direction connected to the rise of support for populist parties across welfare state regimes?

Furthermore, looking into the issue of inequality, labour market development and the loss of jobs have historical roots in welfare state analysis. They seem to be further important parameters for support or not of the development of welfare states. However, they are rarely linked to the reasons why voters in need of welfare state policies might vote for parties with approaches that, in a way, can be argued to not be in their self-interest. This is again related to the literature on voters' attitudes towards welfare development, where self-interest is often seen as an important parameter (Taylor-Gooby and Leruth, 2018). Thus, already, this points to the fact that self-interest can be in one or more areas, and if one set of preferences or disappointment with the development is very strong, this can override the position in the other subsets of voter perceptions as to what will be the best development.

Notes

[1] Data from: www.theatlas.com/charts/Bkmr5DQHW (accessed 12 August 2018).

[2] The results have been online since late October 2017, with updates during 2018.

[3] For a recent update on the development of selected European political parties, see *Economist* (2018), and the data in Appendix 1.

References

Alesina, A., Di Tella, R. and MacCuloch, R. (2004) Inequality and happiness: are Europeans and Americans different? *Journal of Public Economics*, 88: 2009–42.

Autor, D., Dorn, D. and Hanson, G. (2016) The China shock: learning from labor-market adjustment to large changes in trade. *The Annual Review of Economics*, 8: 205–40.

Avent, R. (2017) *The wealth of humans: Work and its absence in the twenty-first century*. London: Penguin Books.

Baumberger, B. (2016) The stigma of claiming benefits: a quantitative study. *Journal of Social Policy*, 45(2): 181–99.

Baute, S., Meuleman, B. and Abts, K. (2018) Welfare state attitudes and support for social Europe: spillover or obstacle? *Journal of Social Policy*, pp 1–19, DOI: 10.1017/S0047279418000314.

Béland, D. (2005) Ideas and social policy: an institutionalist perspective. *Social Policy & Administration*, 39(1): 1–18.

Béland, D. (2018) How ideas impact social policy. In B. Greve (ed) *The Routledge handbook of the welfare state* (2nd edn). Oxon: Routledge, pp 278–87.

Bendz, A. (2017) Empowering the people: public responses to welfare policy change. *Social Policy & Administration*, 51(1): 1–19.

Birnbaum, S., Ferranini, T., Palme, J. and Nelsson, K. (2017) *The generational welfare contract: Justice, institutions and outcomes*. Cheltenham: Edward Elgar.

Cerny, P.G. (1997) Paradoxes of the competition state: the dynamics of political globalisation. *Government and Opposition*, 32(2): 391–418.

Chung, H., Taylor-Gooby, P. and Leruth, B. (2018) Introduction. *Social Policy & Administration*, 52(4): 835–46.

Cingano, F. (2014) Trends in income inequality and its impact on economic growth. OECD Social, Employment and Migration Working Papers, No. 163, Paris.

Dabla-Norris, E., Kochhar, K., Suphaphiphat, N., Ricka, F., Tsounta, E. (2015) Causes and consequences of income inequality: a global perspective. International Monetary Fund, IMF Staff Discussion Note, SDN/15/13.

Doel, H. and Velhoven, B. (1993) *Democracy and welfare economics*. Cambridge: Cambridge University Press.

Downs, A. (1957) An economic theory of political action in a democracy. *Journal of Political Economy*, 65: 135–50.

Economist (2018) Dancing with danger. 3 February.

Esmark, A. and Schoop, S. (2017) Deserving social benefits? Political framing and media framing of 'deservingness' in two welfare reforms in Denmark. *Journal of European Social Policy*, 27(5): 417–32.

Esping-Andersen, G. (1990) *The three worlds of welfare capitalism*. Oxford: Polity Press.

European Commission (2018) *Public opinion in the European Union. Key trends*. Standard Eurobarometer 88, Brussels: European Commission.

European Social Survey (2012) Welfare attitudes in Europe. ESS Topline Results Series, 2nd edition.

Eurostat (2017) Income inequality statistics. Available at: https://ec.europa.eu/eurostat/statistics-explained/index.php?title=Income_poverty_statistics#Income_inequalities

Greve, B. (2017) *Technology and the future of work: The impact on labour markets and welfare states*. Cheltenham: Edward Elgar.

Haidt, J. (2013) *The righteous mind: Why good people are divided by politics and religion*. London: Penguin.

Hochschild, A. (2016) *Strangers in their own land: Anger and mourning on the American Right*. New York, NY: The New Press.

Kahneman, D. (2011) *Thinking, fast and slow*. London: Penguin.

Klein, N. (2017) *No is not enough: Defeating the new shock politics*. London: Allen Lane.

Mason, P. (2016) *Postcapitalism: A guide to our future*. London: Penguin.

Morel, N., Palier, B. and Palme, J. (2012) *Towards a social investment welfare state? Ideas, policies and challenges*. Bristol: Policy Press.

OECD (Organisation for Economic Co-operation and Development) (2017) *Bridging the gap: Inclusive growth 2017 update report*. Paris: OECD.

Oorschot, W. and Roosma, F. (2015) The social legitimacy of differently targeted benefits. Discussion Paper No. 15/11, Improve, Working Papers.

Pickett, K. and Wilkinson, R. (2015) Income inequality and health: a causal review. *Social Science and Medicine*, 128: 316–26.

Piketty, T. (2014) *Capital – in the twenty-first century*. London: Harvard University Press.

Piketty, T. (2016) *Chronicles: On our troubled times*. London: Penguin.

Putnam, R. (2015) *Our kids: The American dream in crisis*. New York, NY: Simon and Schuster.

Romano, S. (2018) *Moralising poverty: The 'undeserving' poor in the public gaze*. Oxon: Routledge.

Roosma, F., Gelissen, J. and Oorschot, W. (2013) The multidimensionality of welfare state attitudes: a European cross-national study. *Social Indicator Research*, 113: 235–55.

Spicker, P. (2018) The real dependent variable problem: the limitations of quantitative analysis in comparative policy studies. *Social Policy & Administration*, 52(1): 218–28.

Taylor-Gooby, P. and Leruth, B. (eds) (2018) *Attitudes, aspirations and welfare: Social policy directions in uncertain times*. Cham: Palgrave Macmillan.

Taylor-Gooby, P., Leruth, B. and Chung, H. (2017) *After Austerity: Welfare state transformation in Europe after the Great Recession*. Oxford: Oxford University Press.

Vance, J.D. (2016) *Hillbilly elegy: A memoir of a family and culture in crisis.* London: William Collins.

Varoufakis, Y. (2017) *And the weak suffer what they must?* London: Vintage.

Watts, B. and Fitzpatrick, S. (2018) *Welfare conditionality.* Oxon: Routledge.

Wilkinson, N. and Klaes, M. (2018) *An introduction to behavioral economics* (3rd edn). London: Macmillan.

Wilkinson, R. and Pickett, K. (2009) *The spirit level – why equality is better for everyone.* London: Allen Lane.

Wilkinson, R. and Pickett, K. (2018) *The inner level: How more equal societies reduce stress, restore sanity and improve everyone's well-being.* St. Ives: Allen Lane.

Winlow, S., Hall, S. and Treadwell, J. (2017) *The rise of the Right: English nationalism and the transformation of working-class politics.* Bristol: Policy Press.

Yerkes, M. and Peper, B. (2018) Welfare states and the life course. In B. Greve (ed) *Handbook of the welfare state* (2nd edn). Oxon: Routledge, pp 92–100.

2

Basic concepts

Introduction

Voters' and citizens' perception of what would be the best way for a welfare state to develop are often analysed using a variety of concepts. These concepts are presented, albeit briefly, as this helps to frame the understanding, analysis and discussion in the book. The basic concepts that are discussed and presented in this chapter are: welfare chauvinism, legitimacy, deserving/undeserving, populism and ideas.

The central reason for choosing these concepts is that several of them are not always used consistently and/or have connotations that implicitly indicate a normative position. Furthermore, they can be used as a way to understand the arguments and reasons for people's positions across welfare states. This is also because these concepts are influential – some for many years – in the understanding of why welfare states have developed as they have. Lastly, one can argue that social policy (and welfare state development) is dependent to a large degree on demand and broad political support (Rehm, 2011).

The chapter starts, in the next section, with what is populism as this is one of the most discussed aspects of societal development in recent years linking ideas and social policy. The core reason for this is that populism and populist ideas are embedded in the development of most welfare states, often even without having been presented as such. This is followed by presenting how ideas, such as populist ideas, can influence societal development. Historically, the legitimacy of welfare states has also been on the agenda and this is probed into in the fourth section, especially as Chapter 7 looks into attitudes towards, and the legitimacy of, the welfare state. Welfare chauvinism is a relatively new concept and might also be considered a populist idea, which also catches many of the different aspects looked at earlier in the chapter. Thereby, it is a useful concept as a way of summing up the possible impact on welfare state development. This is looked at further in the fifth section, before the sixth section concludes the chapter.

Populism

Populism has been on the agenda for some years now, and several political groupings and activists have been argued to be populist movements, from Occupy Wall Street to the Tea Party in the US, and in Europe especially, several right-wing parties are argued to be populist (Mudde, 2004), although there are also populist parties on the Left, where South America has especially been mentioned as having examples thereof. It has been defined in many ways, ranging from a style, a discourse, an organisational form to an ideology (Rooduijn and Pauwels, 2011). The restructuring of welfare states has also been argued to be a reason for increased populism, especially against immigrants as part of reduced social cohesion (Boucher, 2017).

Populism is, in a way, a simple word that lends explanation to itself – it is, in one way or another, something that, for some, is popular. The *Oxford English dictionary* has the following definition:

> The policies or principles of any of various political parties which seek to represent the interests of ordinary people, *spec.* of the Populists of the U.S. or Russia. Also: support for or representation of ordinary people or their views; speech, action, writing, etc., intended to have general appeal.[1]

Another definition, referring back to Rousseau, is as follows:

> populism as a thin-centered ideology that considers society to be ultimately separated into two homogenous and antagonistic camps, 'the pure people' versus 'the corrupt elite', and which argues that politics should be an expression of the volontè gènèrale (general will) of the people. (Mudde and Cristóbal, 2017: 703)

The issue of the dialectic between elites and the people is returned to later. Although often described as related to a group of people or a broader set of actors, it can also be defined as follows: 'populism is best defined as a political strategy through which personalistic leader seeks or exercises government based on direct, unmediated, uninstitutionalized support from large number of mostly unorganized followers' (Weyland, 2001, cited in Anselmi, 2018: 45). In this definition is added a person who has leadership – or, one could argue, charisma – being able to make people believe in what can be good for society and their own personal development, which can thus build up to improvements in or maintaining the status quo if that is best for the individual, or at least they are led to believe so. This presumably also supports welfare chauvinism (see later).

Overall, it can be considered that populists have four characteristics in common:

1. emphasising the central position of the people;
2. criticising the elite;
3. seeing the people as a homogeneous group; and
4. dealing with serious crises (Rooduijn, 2014).

Whether populism only increases in times of crisis can be questioned, but the three other aspects run through much of the analysis of what populism is.

Populism can also be seen both as a political battle term – a short way to argue that an opponent is just saying something to get votes – and also as a very vague term. It has therefore been used in many and very different connotations, ranging from irresponsible economic policy to why those against globalisation and migration pursue populist approaches. The quest for power in democracies can, in a way, also be argued to have populist traits, meaning that, to a certain extent, all parties try to get as many votes as possible by having viewpoints that can engender broader support. Historically, it has also been framed as a way of getting support from the silent majority in order for the populists themselves to be in power (Mudde and Cristóbal, 2017). In modern times, President Nixon in the US is such an example (Isenberg, 2017). Overall, the core of the populism story is thus that populists represent the people and their true will (Müller, 2016).

This has also, in general, given rise to debate on the elite versus the layman (the ordinary people). This debate is old:

> Socrates argued that society was ready to defer to the views of experts and ignore the opinion of ordinary folk on technical matters such as shipbuilding and architecture, and he was at a loss as to why the same approach was not adopted in relation to political life. (Furedi, 2018: 126)

This also indicates that populism is often seen by some as the discussion of how to integrate knowledge in decision-making while, at the same time, accepting and using liberal-democratic values, where those electing (or voting in referendums) are those who have the formal right to make the decisions. Therefore, populists will often 'detest the political establishment, but they also critique the economic elite, the cultural elite, and the media elite' (Mudde and Cristóbal, 2017: 793). Questions related to the elite also help in explaining the often negative attitudes, such as the negative stance towards the European Union (EU). Many populist parties in Europe see the EU as far away and taking decisions without including the viewpoints of local people. This might thereby also be part of the reason for Brexit. Still, it can also be argued that:

> the heart of populism concerns the conflict between, on the one hand, the mythical, homogenous and unified common people and, on the other hand, an enemy that consists of a divisive political, economic and cultural elite, to which very often a dangerous and threatening 'other' is added. (Schumacher and Kersbergen, 2016: 302)

Besides topics and suggestions for changes, a difference between left- and right-wing populism could be that right-wing populism, other than the elite versus people approach, also has a focus not only on up and down the hierarchy, but also on a specific group (Judis, 2016); in recent years, this has often been immigrants and refugees. Methodologically, it can be difficult as the indicators are based on averages and the reason for supporting populist parties can vary; thereby, aggregate data might hide relationships. This is the reason why a number of studies cannot necessarily point to, for example, unemployment being the reason for support for right-wing populist parties (Amengay and Stockemer, 2018). Overall, this points to a debate between insiders and outsiders, natives and aliens, but also a struggle for power. Often, this is influenced by ideas (see later).

In general, in Western Europe and the US, there has been a rise in support for populist parties (Schumacher and Kersbergen, 2016), which also makes it important to ensure an understanding of what populism and populist parties are, even though they might and will differ across countries. There need not be the same types of populist party around the world as they can be anti-euro and anti-immigrant in Europe, anti-trade in the US, and Left populist in Latin America, with a long tradition back to Peron in Argentine (Rodrik, 2017).

Populism is here understood in its broad connotation of strategies aiming to help gain support for political parties and make it possible to influence policy development and have power in a country through the use of specific policy platforms – in particular, in this book, welfare chauvinism. Given the difficulties in measuring populism, which have been analysed only to a limited extent (Rooduijn and Pauwels, 2011), this is not the aim in the following, where the focus is more upon how this can have an influence on the legitimacy of welfare states (see later and Chapter 7). One can further argue that all parties wanting to gain power need to have some traits of populism, although it cannot be shown that mainstream parties have adopted populist viewpoints (Rooduijn et al, 2014). This information was based upon a content analysis in five Western countries; still, it might be that it has an impact over time and, further, that the degree of impact will depend upon the electoral system (eg in the UK system, first-past-the-post elections make it difficult for new parties to gain seats in Parliament). However, major parties might still adopt part of the agendas of populist groups or parties (Judis, 2016).

Modern populism is different from 'the [early] socialists, who want[ed] to "uplift the workers" by re-educating them, thereby liberating them from their "false-consciousness"' (Mudde, 2004: 547). However, it still seems to be a question of information and misinformation that is an issue today (Kuklinski et al, 2000).

Populists might also have influence because they, as in the median voter model, might be able to veto or block decisions. This can then be used to support the agenda that they want to have on the table. They might have further influence due to the fact that disadvantaged groups have reduced political efficacy, and therefore policies reducing this, such as social investment, might reduce support for populist parties (Marx and Nguyen, 2018).

Ideas

Ideas have always had, and will presumably continue to have, an impact on societal development, although it has been, and will most likely also continue to be, difficult to measure and find the exact impact of ideas on welfare state developments. An early study indicated that ideological factors could influence support for welfare policies (Blekesaune and Quadagno, 2003). Ideas might not be the same in all countries, and the support for governmental intervention as one such factor is thus stronger in Europe than in the US (Svallfors, 2014).

'Ideas can be simply defined as the causal and normative beliefs held by social and policy actors' (Béland and Mahon, 2016: 43). Béland (2019) has also pointed to how ideas shape actors' perceptions. They also matter because framing suggestions and policies can influence the policy process and policy cycle; thus, one needs to look into the policy stream, agenda-setting, alternatives and paradigms (Béland, 2005, 2016).

Here, the central focus is on the concept of ideas with an eye to welfare state development. Related to populism (see earlier), it is important to be aware that some of the aims and goals of welfare policies can have similarities despite the fact that 'they tend to have different underlying ideas about the causes of unemployment, inequality and poverty' (Peters, 2015: 77). This is important because parts of the debates on welfare state development revolve around these exact aspects, and how they influence people's everyday lives (on inequality and the impact of the development on the labour market, see also Chapters 3 and 4).

Part of the way in which ideas can influence the development is that presenting ideas might be a way to try to set the agenda for change and/or the continuation of welfare state development. Thus, this also points to the fact that being an agenda-setter can have an impact on possible policy development as this can influence policies used to attract voters. However, it can be difficult to set an agenda without having an idea about what is important and why this issue should be part of the discussion. Ideas do not just have influence out of the blue; rather, they are part of the process of making decisions, including changing legal and economic structures. Therefore, as often argued by populist parties, ideas and related policies can be presented as a 'them and us' problem, or the elite versus the people, so that ideas that can be shown or be argued to support the people can have a stronger impact than other ideas if populism influences development. This might, however, be misused to pursue an agenda that de facto causes better living conditions for those already well off, for example, by reducing taxation on the rich in order that this should support the poor in the longer run through trickle-down effects (see also Chapter 3).

Sometimes, a change in ideas follows factors influencing the standard of living of many, including rising unemployment. The change in welfare states since the first oil-price crisis (1972/73), and what followed in the industrialised world of stagflation (stagnating economies and high levels of inflation) and an increase in unemployment, caused the question to be asked of the effectiveness of Keynesian demand management for welfare state developments. Until the crisis, Keynesian ideas were seen as core ideas framing welfare state development in many countries and also the expansion of welfare states. Instead, a more neoliberal agenda with less focus on state intervention gained ground.

Ideas in themselves influence voters' perception of what a good social policy is, as do decision-makers themselves when presenting suggestions. This can be in the form of the impact of public positions and papers from think tanks, among others. Think tanks can, for example, act as pressure groups in favour of the expansion of social policy in general or for a specific part of social policy, but can also, as neoliberal think tanks often do, argue in favour of the reduction of social policy as a way to be able to reduce taxes and duties (see also Chapter 4).

Changes in ideas might also be the result of specific groups' self-interest. This includes pressure groups that are employed in certain sectors of the welfare state which argue that if they receive more money, then they can deliver better welfare, and can improve well-being in society. In most cases, it will be possible to deliver a higher level of quality if more money is available; still, society will have to prioritise among different aims and options (see more in Chapter 5). This is because there might also be steering problems in ensuring that society gets value for money. This problem is often labelled the principal–agent problem, where the principal is the financier of an activity, which is delivered by the agent. It might be difficult for the principal to know what exactly the agent delivers and whether more could be expected for the given sum of money. This explains why a demand for more money is not always accepted, but also why the principal often wants to measure and have information on the outcome of spending money within an area, and the ability to argue that more or less money can be important for the people can have an impact on their political support.

Self-interest theory revolves around the fact that those actually receiving benefits and/or services, or who have family/friends already getting it or just about to get it, are often more supportive of the specific welfare benefit (Taylor-Gooby et al, 2018). A concrete example is that 'individual differences in childcare support among European parents are driven by interest, ideologies and assessments of current provision' (Chung and Meuleman, 2017: 61). Self-interest as a driver for change can be pursued by welfare chauvinism (Jæger, 2006; Lubbers et al, 2018; see also later). This also helps in explaining the often high level of support for elderly care (we all hope to be old) and health care as even behind the veil of ignorance (Rawls, 1971), when we cross to the other side of the veil if we are sick or in need of treatment, we would be sure that this would be the best possible care. Studies often also confirm general support for the elderly before the sick and the unemployed, although with differences among welfare states and dependent on socio-economic conditions (Laenen and Meuleman, 2017).

Naturally, some ideas are first presented or able to influence development when there is what has been labelled a window of opportunity (Kingdon, 1984), such as the first and second oil crises, as argued earlier. A window of opportunity can have different forms, but it can, for example, be a financial crisis, making it more legitimate to reduce the level of benefits than it would be in times of good economic options. In times of crisis, it might thus be more possible to introduce austerity policies in a neoliberal way (see more on the data and whether this has been the case in Chapter 5), whereas in good economic times, it can be more difficult to persuade the electorate that these are necessary policies. The use of language can also influence social policy development (Béland and Petersen, 2014), for example, the use of different connotations of migrants and their access to welfare benefits can influence the discourse and the willingness to pay for benefits if, in this case, migrants have access to these benefits. Thereby, an increase in migration can also, in this way, be a window of opportunity for populist parties to gain votes. Making a distinction between them (the others) and us is also a way of influencing perceptions about who should have benefits, under what conditions and how generous the benefits should be. Thereby, influencing the understanding of who does and does not deserve benefits can influence support to and the legitimacy of the welfare state (see also later).

In relation to welfare states, it is often argued that three paradigms in particular have been influential in welfare state development: Keynesian, neoliberal and social investment. These are not presented in detail here (see, instead, Greve, 2015), but there is a strong contrast between the understanding of the role of the state between the Keynesian and neoliberal paradigms, where Keynesianism would have a stronger role for the state than neoliberalism (on social investment, see Morel et al, 2012).

Even in a rational understanding, ideas have influence as even 'preferences, constraints, and choice variables – rely on an implicit set of ideas' (Rodrik, 2014: 191). Interest can also be understood as an idea in itself, and individuals' ideas might also influence their perceived identity and related changes. Attitudes towards the welfare state might even be more influenced by ideas than by self-interest (Roosma et al, 2012), and this can include ideas about the cost of services and the actual behaviour of those receiving benefits (Taylor-Gooby et al, 2018). Ideas that can be argued to have a populist trait relate to people-centrism, anti-elitism, homogeneity of the people, direct democracy, exclusionism and proclamation of a crisis (Rooduijun, 2014); as presented earlier, populism uses these ideas to gain support.

Legitimacy in general and who is deserving

The legitimacy of the welfare state has, by now, been on the agenda for a long time. In general, this revolves around two different, but highly interlinked, issues. The 'old' debate was about the ability to finance the welfare state (Offe, 1984). In addition to this were debates about whether the welfare state was too expensive given the goals it achieved (Klein, 1993; ISSA, 1995), and thus also whether there was too much bureaucracy in the administration of the welfare state. From what, at that time, was argued to be the New Right were arguments that the welfare state had grown too much due to politicians' inability to cope with pressure groups. This can especially be found in the theoretical approach of public choice (Niskanen, 1971; Mueller, 1987). Overall, it was argued that there was a crisis in the welfare state (for an early argument, see OECD, 1981), and to such an extent that it was also perceived as an intellectual crisis for welfare state development (Alber, 1988). Even before discussions on austerity and permanent retrenchment (Pierson, 2001), overall debates on welfare state development indicate that the discussions were about what the welfare state should do (for an early review of this literature, see Starke, 2006). Thus – and the reason for the quotation marks around 'old' at the beginning of this paragraph – crisis and change in the support for the welfare state, which reflect the legitimacy of the welfare state in different ways, are not new issues. Therefore, for a long time, there have been discussions, often with different names, understandings and approaches, as to how society should and could develop. In the 1980s and 1990s, the issues of new technology and globalisation were also on the agenda, although, seemingly, not with a strong and negative perception of the tasks that the welfare state should do. However, as presented in Chapter 5, there is empirically only limited support for the permanent austerity approach. The focus on output legitimacy (eg the ability to help citizens in line with their self-interest and values) is important, and points to legitimacy being important as a way of understanding trust in public institutions (as discussed later in Chapter 7), and perhaps even generalised social trust (Jann, 2016). Another hypothesis related to trust is that immigration might lead to a lower level of trust and solidarity due to the fact that people might believe that an increasing share of benefits goes to immigrants (Ervasti and Hjerm, 2012).

In the same vein as the second issue is the discussion on who does and does not deserve benefits and services from the welfare state. This is also a rather old topic related to welfare state developments, although it is still argued that opinions on social policy are strongly influenced by whether or not recipients are seen as deserving, but also that it can and will be different for different parts of the welfare state (Jensen and Petersen, 2017). Also, it has long been known that migrants are often seen as less deserving (Van Oorschot, 2006). The distinction between 'them' and 'us' can thus be used as part of an idea to change welfare states by pointing to the legitimacy of benefits. Principles for welfare redistribution can also influence the perception of who is deserving, so that merit (those who contribute should receive) and need (those in highest need) count as central issues (Jørgensen and Thomsen, 2016).

Related to legitimacy and who does and does not deserve is a discussion on whether there is just use of the benefit systems, or, in fact, a high level of misuse, even labelled the Achilles' heel of welfare state legitimacy (Roosma et al, 2016). The discussion points to the fact that, based on data from 2008, the perceptions of voters, which seem to be prevalent in all European countries, indicate that the understanding of overuse is more influenced by ideology, whereas underuse is more influenced by issues such as structure and level and size of unemployment. This might be because underuse 'can be unintentional, e.g., resulting from ignorance of social rights, or intentional, e.g., when a benefit is not claimed for fear of stigmatization' (Roosma et al, 2016: 178), with the situation being that in Southern and Eastern Europe, underuse perceptions are strong, whereas the overuse understanding is more prevalent in Anglo-Saxon countries (Geiger, 2018).

The fact that voters' perceptions do not necessarily conform to the actual development and size of benefits and/or level of services is not new. In the UK, for example, it looks like the level of benefits is overestimated: 'for unemployment benefits, noticeably more people in recent years overestimate the benefit than underestimate it (8–11 per cent more for a single woman, 27–28 per cent more for a childless couple' (Geiger, 2018: 1010). People in favour of a strong role for the welfare state can find that the performance is either bad or good, but the opposite can also be the case, so that those preferring a weak welfare state can have a critical role of what is done if the performance is good, but if the perceived performance is bad, then they might be critical overall (Roosma et al, 2014). Further, it seems that support, for example, for the state having a role in ensuring jobs is less strong than it used to be, and even 'support for right-wing populism seems bound to rise as electorates continue to hold national politicians accountable for their growing sense of insecurity and socio-economic misfortune' (Deeming, 2018: 1119). This is in line with another study which shows that active labour market policies are implemented despite limited support (Fossati, 2018).

Perceptions can also be formed by false beliefs and, based upon a US study, it might even be the case that many of those who overestimate state spending on welfare are also those who most believe that their knowledge is correct (Kuklinski et al, 2000). Perceptions can further be influenced by the position in society, so that, for example, temporary workers might have different preferences than those at the core of the labour market (Marx, 2015). Naturally, the perception of who is in need and the size of support that they are entitled to can be influenced by biases in knowledge and the anchoring of values to benefits, which might help in explaining discretion and even professional judgements in the welfare states (Molander, 2016). Molander further argues that in relation to the delivery of welfare service, discretion cannot be eliminated. It also seems that the ability to influence people's perceptions, at least with regard to sanctioning, will influence how this is framed, so that moral arguments related to well-being might have a stronger impact on legitimacy than economic arguments (Kootstra and Roosma, 2018). The fact that framing is important is not surprising; however, it also indicates why some people continue to have specific viewpoints on the government's role and legitimacy (see more in Chapter 6).

Legitimacy therefore revolves around who gets the benefits/services and whether the welfare state is seen as efficient. This further implies that if there is a strong negative perception that the undeserving are receiving benefits, then a person can, despite being in favour of a strong welfare state, have a negative stance on part of it. It has also been argued that support to the middle class has been one of the aspects in ensuring legitimacy and gaining support from the middle class as they have been seen as the class that could swing the majority from one side to the other, for example, a kind of median voter argument (Mau, 2015). Austerity has, at the same time, been argued to undermine support to the middle class (Taylor-Gooby et al, 2017), therefore opening the way to reduce the legitimacy and support for welfare state development in the longer term.

Working-class/middle-class welfare is also a type of self-interest argument, which 'implies that the elderly or older middle-aged population should be more likely to support public programs for the elderly, but less likely to support programs for children' (Blekesaune and Quadagno, 2003: 416); thus, the middle class will also support the welfare state if they gain from it themselves. This is because 'low-risk citizens – whose support is critical for a generous benefit regime, have few incentives to be part of a common risk pool, simply because they subsidize their higher-risk countrymen' (Rehm, 2011: 272). The acceptance of a more neoliberal approach in some countries is argued to be due to Mau's idea that 'the up-and-coming and increasingly materially saturated middle class lost sight of the original' (Mau, 2015: xi). Mau further argues that the middle class became comfortable with the market's provision of social services. Another possible issue is that the middle class 'tends to prefer social investment and activation over traditional redistributive policies' (Gingrich and Häuserman, 2015: 51). In principle, this is contradictory to low-income groups' need for economic security, and further means that the working class has lower support for traditional left-wing parties supporting welfare expansion, while, at the same time, there has been increasing support from some populist right-wing parties to specific parts of welfare state development. Overall, this points to the fact that if self-interest is central, whether generalised or reciprocal, this implies the risk of a contradiction in welfare states and reduces legitimacy in times of different kinds of external shocks to the state's ability to finance and develop welfare states (Rehm et al, 2012).

One issue that might have a strong impact on trust and legitimacy in welfare states seems to be labour market insecurity. Based upon analysis of the first six rounds of the European Social Survey, labour market insecurity has a negative impact on social trust, although 'atypical employment does not correlate with reduced trust' (Nguyen, 2017: 230). Still, as will also be witnessed in Chapter 6, the issue of insecurity and loss of jobs has an impact on support for populist opinion.

The fact that there can be differences in ideas of justice and approaches to, and types of, redistribution might also influence the legitimacy of the welfare state. Some might prefer that merit has a strong influence; others that need should be strong. However, there does not seem to be a common understanding in Europe (based on data for 2008), and, further, it varies across different social risks and social programmes (Reeskens and van Oorschot, 2013).

Part of the legitimacy and support for welfare states might also rest on a variation of normative perceptions of undeserving people who receive welfare benefits, who are given names such as 'black', 'welfare queen', 'lazy unemployed' and, lately, 'immigrants' (van Oorschot and Roosma, 2015). In public debates, these groups (along with others termed 'parasites' and 'scroungers') have often been used as scapegoats for changes (Romano, 2018).

The relation between the design of the institutional structure and legitimacy is contested, so it is difficult to be sure of the causality (Laenen, 2018), although this does not change the fact that support depends on perceptions of self-interest and deservingness. This also implies that trust in the government and institutional structures also influences the degree of legitimacy (van Oorschot et al, 2017). Immigrants often come low on the scale of deservingness (Taylor-Gooby and Leruth, 2018).

Overall, therefore, in simple terms, legitimacy is whether voters find that they get what they have been promised with a sufficient high quality at a reasonable price, for example, the level of tax to pay. Also, overall, there is support for health care and the elderly, but less so for social assistance, unemployment benefits and active labour market policies. Naturally, individual attitudes are influenced by different welfare states and contextual factors, but also by how rich a country is (Roosma and van Oorschot, 2017).

Welfare chauvinism

Welfare chauvinism can be argued to be a political view in which nativism should be a central principle, by which is meant that welfare benefits and services should mainly go to national citizens (Ennser-Jedenastik, 2018), and, even further, to only those persons. Framing of who is deserving/undeserving can thus also influence social policy (Giger, 2017).

The trend in countries towards stronger electoral support for populist parties (Schumacher and Kersbergen, 2016), including those with a welfare chauvinist agenda, might partly be driven by catchwords such as 'welfare tourism' and 'welfare magnetism', which both relate to the free movement of workers within the EU. There is a conflict here within the EU member states (typically, an east–west divide) between sending and receiving countries, but there is also a clash of 'supporters of pan-European free-movement and non-discrimination, on the one hand, against supporters of social and cultural closures, on the other' (Ferrera, 2017: 7). It further includes the wider issue of international migration and refugees and their access to welfare benefits and services, and the last refugee crisis of 2015/16 caused increased criticisms of possible welfare tourism. In a sense, although not often framed in this way, this reflects viewpoints on the deserving/undeserving as presented earlier, so that natives are the deserving, whereas this is not the case for migrants/refugees, and often also those who are not seen to be working hard. Besides economic reasons, it can also be due to cultural and social values that low-income groups have a welfare chauvinistic approach, including having a more authoritarian ideological understanding; therefore, 'perceived threat by outgroups is pivotal to understanding how authoritarian dispositions might translate into outgroup hostility' (Mewes and Mau, 2014: 125).

Attitudes towards different kinds of need or who is deserving might change over time and vary across countries, with the lowest support in the US and the highest in several European countries (Deeming, 2018). Reflection on attitudes to and reasons for inequality might also have an impact (Alesina et al, 2004). This might also help in explaining that even though overall retrenchment seems to have a negative impact on support for a government, this seems not to be the case for changes in the unemployment benefit system (Giger, 2017).

One peculiarity is that while welfare chauvinism might be one issue, part of the rhetoric has also been that some people might be welfare 'scroungers', that is, they misuse the system. They might, in fact, be native, implying that there can be natives who are 'misusing' the system, not only migrants. This can be an important perspective as, for example, part of the Brexit debate was about benefits, migrants and the impact of globalisation (Taylor-Gooby, 2017). In fact, across Europe (although with data from 2008), 'the European public is unanimous across regions in their perception of substantial abuse of welfare benefits' (Roosma and van Oorschot, 2017: 712).

In general, welfare chauvinism seems to be an important aspect of populist right-wing parties as they will demonstrate greater opposition to 'social programs that are in conflict with this goal, or advocate changes to programs in order to make them conform to it' (Ensser-Jedenastik, 2018: 297). At the same time, the support for welfare to natives implies that populist right-wing parties – which, in principle, could prefer to reduce the size of the welfare state, including a reduction in taxes and duties – might support the expansion of the welfare state if they can rest assured that those benefitting from it will mainly be their own voters. There are, however, differences among welfare regimes, so that 'in countries with the most selective welfare regimes, the native population is the most welfare chauvinistic' (Waal et al, 2013: 175). The fact that populist parties support policies in order to gain votes is, naturally, not so different from other parties' approaches aiming to get the largest support at elections. However, the quest for more welfare for some and less for others causes difficulties in depicting and finding reasons for populist parties' ways of acting in different countries, and presumably also in relation to the legitimacy of the welfare state (see also Chapter 7). Mainstream parties might try to argue for part of the same, thus indicating a reason that support for populist parties varies across countries. It also seems that 'the social policy positions of populist right parties seem to be more inclined towards a revival than a dismantling of the welfare state' (Fenger, 2018: 18).

However, at the same time, if voters' strongest preference is against migrants, then what the party they support does in other spheres of political life might be less important to them. In line with the classical median voter model (Downs, 1957), it can be difficult to predict outcomes as there are so many issues at stake, and for some voters, one specific issue might trump all the others. This could be part of the reason why voters who could gain from redistribution in principle vote for parties where this will not be the most likely outcome of their activities (see also Chapters 3 and 4). Thus, if those voting for parties with a welfare chauvinist agenda, and who are against migration, are also the voters who can change the balance from one group of parties to another group, then this might influence several policy areas at the same time. As already argued earlier, mainstream parties might also adapt to the agenda of populist parties in order to continue to gain votes; therefore, at an overall level, 'the median voter model is a good approximation of demand aggregation in the public sector for many issues' (Holcombe, 1989: 123). As such, even relatively small groups with a welfare chauvinistic agenda can, in certain circumstances, influence societies' development.

It is also the case that 'ethnic citizenship attitudes were related with more positive attitudes on welfare, but also with increased welfare chauvinism' (Vandoninck et al, 2018: 171). Therefore, there is a relation between welfare benefits, economic options and culture and national identity, especially when immigration is seen as a central topic (Keskinen et al, 2016). It seems that in all European countries (based on data from 2008), immigrants are seen as less deserving than native populations (Waal et al, 2013), which supports a movement towards a more welfare chauvinistic policy approach, possibly becoming even stronger in the wake of the increasing number of migrants and refugees in recent years.

It is not clear whether populism is a stronger challenge for some welfare states than others, but it has been assumed that universal welfare states would be more threatened than social insurance welfare regimes (Ennser-Jedenastik, 2018), although this does not seem to fit fully with the very diverse country developments in Europe. However, if populism is a reaction to a perceived threat of one's own values, as well as anti-establishment feeling (Anselmi, 2018), then this could also lead to welfare chauvinism. Thus, even policies to promote equal rights related to gender, ethnicity and/or sexual preferences might be seen as threatening a group of persons. To summarise, welfare chauvinism is here understood as support for welfare state policies that help in ensuring that natives have the best access to welfare benefits and services.

Conclusion

This chapter has presented the core concepts that are used throughout the book, including ideas, populism, legitimacy and welfare chauvinism. It further indicated that aspects of populism and welfare chauvinism might help in explaining changes in welfare states and the possible impact thereof with regard to how welfare states develop, and also the legitimacy of welfare states. It is, however, important to be aware of the fact that how to measure the direct impact between the core concepts is not simple and straightforward as the counterfactual situation in reality does not exist.

The chapter also emphasised how ideas can influence societal development as this can have an impact on political decision-makers, but also on voters' stances on what is important for societies' development. Thus, these concepts can presumably help in understanding some of the changes in welfare states in recent years. This also includes the legitimacy of welfare states. Historically, this has also been an important issue given that welfare states without legitimacy will be more open to major changes, including reductions and retrenchment, albeit not necessarily in all areas, but more selected areas, and even with possible expansion in others (see more in Chapter 3). Legitimacy is a central aspect of Chapter 7.

Note

1 See: Oxford English Dictionary, www.oed.com.ep.fjernadgang. kb.dk/view/Entry/147930?redirectedFrom=populism#eid (accessed 8 November 2017 through Roskilde University Library).

References

Alber, J. (1988) Continuities and change in the idea of the welfare state. *Politics and Society*, 16(4): 451–68.

Alesina, A., Di Tella, R. and MacCuloch, R. (2004) Inequality and happiness: are Europeans and Americans different? *Journal of Public Economics*, 88: 2009–42.

Amengay, A. and Stockemer, D. (2018) The Radical Right in Western Europe: a meta-analysis of structural factors. *Political Studies Review*, pp 1–21, DOI: 10.117/147892991877975.

Anselmi, M. (2018) *Populism: An introduction*. Oxon: Routledge.

Béland, D. (2005) Ideas and social policy: an institutionalist perspective. *Social Policy & Administration*, 39(1): 1–18.

Béland, D. (2016) Ideas and institutions in social policy research. *Social Policy & Administration*, 50(6): 734–50.

Béland, D. (2018) How ideas impact social policy. In B. Greve (ed) *The Routledge handbook of the welfare state* (2nd edn). Oxon: Routledge, pp 278–87.

Béland, D. and Mahon, R. (2016) *Advanced introduction to social policy*. Cheltenham: Edward Elgar.

Béland, D. and Petersen, K. (2014) *Analysing social policy concepts and language*. Bristol: Policy Press.

Blekesaune, M. and Quadagno, J. (2003) Public attitudes toward welfare state policies: a comparative analysis of 24 nations. *European Sociological Review*, 19(5): 415–27.

Boucher, G. (2017) European social cohesions. In G. Boucher and Y. Samad (eds) *Social cohesion and social change in Europe*. Oxon: Routledge.

Chung, H. and Meuleman, B. (2017) European parents' attitudes towards public childcare provision: the role of current provisions, interest and ideologies, *European Societies*, 19(1): 49–68.

Deeming, C. (2018) The politics of (fractured) solidarity: a cross-national analysis of class bases of the welfare state. *Social Policy & Administration*, 52(5): 1106–25.

Downs, A. (1957) An economic theory of political action in a democracy. *Journal of Political Economy*, 65: 135–50.

Ennser-Jedenastik, L. (2018) Welfare chauvinism in populist Radical Right platforms: the role of redistributive justice principles. *Social Policy & Administration*, 52(1): 293–314.

Ervasti, H. and Hjerm, M. (2012) Immigration, trust and support for the welfare state. In H. Ervasti, J.G. Andersen, T. Fridberg and K. Ringdahl (eds) *The future of the welfare state: Social policy attitudes and social capital in Europe*. Cheltenham: Edward Elgar.

Fenger, M. (2018) The social policy agendas of populist Radical Right parties in comparative perspective. *Journal of International and Comparative Social Policy*, pp 1–22, DOI: 10.1080/21699763.2018.1483255.

Ferrera, M. (2017) The Stein Rokkan lecture 2016. Mission impossible? Reconciling economic and social Europe after the euro crisis and Brexit. *European Journal of Political Research*, 56(3): 3–22.

Fossati, F. (2018) Who wants demanding active labour market policies? Public attitudes towards policies that put pressure on the unemployed. *Journal of Social Policy*, 47(1): 77–97.

Furedi, F. (2018) *Populism and the European culture wars. The conflict of values between Hungary and the EU*. Oxon: Routledge.

Geiger, B.B. (2018) Benefit 'myths'? The accuracy and inaccuracy of public beliefs about the benefits system. *Social Policy & Administration*, 52: 998–1018, DOI: 10.1111/spol.12347.

Giger, N. (2017) *The risk of social policy? The electoral consequence of welfare state retrenchment and social policy performance in OECD-countries*. Cheltenham: Edward Elgar.

Gingrich, J. and Häusermann, S. (2015) The decline of the working-class vote, the reconfiguration of the welfare support coalition and consequences for the welfare state. *Journal of European Social Policy*, 25(1): 50–75.

Greve, B. (2015) *Welfare and the welfare state: Present and future*. London: Routledge, DOI: 10.4324/9781315761022.

Holcombe, R. (1989) The median voter model in public choice theory. *Public Choice*, 61: 115–25.

Isenberg, N. (2017) *White trash*. London: Atlantic Books.

ISSA (International Social Security Association) (1995) *Social security tomorrow: Permanence and change*. Geneva: International Social Security Association.

Jæger, M. (2006) What makes people support public responsibility for welfare provision: self-interest or political ideology? A longitudinal approach. *Acta Sociologica*, 49(3): 321–38.

Jann, W. (2016) Accountability, performance and the legitimacy in the welfare state. If accountability is the answer, what was the question? In T. Cristensen and P. Lægreid (eds) *The Routledge handbook to accountability and welfare state reforms in Europe*. Oxon: Routledge.

Jensen, C. and Petersen, M. (2017) The deservingness heuristic and the politics of health care. *American Journal of Political Science*, 61(1): 68–83.

Jørgensen, M. and Thomsen, T. (2016) Deservingness in the Danish context: Welfare chauvinism in times of crisis. *Critical Social Policy*, 36(3): 330–51.

Judis, J. (2016) *The populist explosion: How the Great Recession transformed American and European politics.* New York, NY: Columbia Global Reports.

Keskinen, S., Norcel, O. and Jørgensen, M. (2016) The politics and policies of welfare chauvinism under the economic crisis. *Critical Social Policy*, 36(3): 321–9.

Kingdon, J. (1984) *Agendas, alternatives and public policies.* Boston, MA: Little Brown Book.

Klein, R. (1993) O'Goffe's tale. In C. Jones (ed) *New perspectives on the welfare state in Europe.* London: Routledge.

Kootstra, A. and Roosma, F. (2018) Changing public support for welfare sanctioning in Britain and the Netherlands: A persuasion experiment. *Social Policy & Administration*, 52(4): 847–61.

Kuklinski, J., Quirk, P.J., Jerit, J., Schwieder, D. and Rich, R.F. (2000) Misinformation and the currency of democratic citizenship. *The Journal of Politics*, 62(3): 790–816.

Laenen, T. (2018) Do institutions matter? The interplay between income benefit design, popular perceptions, and the social legitimacy of targeted welfare. *Journal of European Social Policy*, 28(1): 4–17.

Laenen, T. and Meuleman, B. (2017) A universal rank order of deservingness? Geographical, temporal and socio-structural comparisons. In W. van Oorschot, F. Roosma, B. Meuleman and T. Reeskens (eds) *The social legitimacy of targeted welfare. Attitudes to welfare deservingness.* Cheltenham: Edward Elgar.

Lubbers, M., Diehl, C., Kuhn, T., Larsen, C.A. et al (2018) Migrants' support for welfare state spending in Denmark, Germany and the Netherlands. *Social Policy & Administration*, 52(4): 895–913.

Marx, P. (2015) *The political behaviour of temporary workers.* Houndmills: Palgrave Macmillan.

Marx, P. and Nguyen, C. (2018) Political participation in European welfare states: does social investment matter? *Journal of European Public Policy*, 25(6): 912–43.

Mau, S. (2015) *Inequality, marketization and the majority class: Why did the European middle classes accept neo-liberalism?* Houndsmills: Palgrave Macmillan.

Mewes, J. and Mau, S. (2014) Unraveling working-class welfare chauvinism. In S. Svallfors (ed) *Welfare attitudes and beyond.* Stanford, CA: Stanford University Press.

Molander, A. (2016) *Discretion in the welfare state. Social rights and professional judgment.* Oxon: Routledge.

Morel, N., Palier, B. and Palme, J. (2012) *Towards a social investment welfare state? Ideas, policies and challenges.* Bristol: Policy Press.

Mudde, C. (2004) *The populist zeitgeist, government and opposition.* Oxford: Blackwell.

Mudde, C. and Cristóbal, R. (2017) *Populism: A very short introduction.* Oxford: Oxford University Press.

Mueller, D. (1987) *The growth of government: A public choice perspective.* Staff paper, New York, NY: IMF.

Müller, J. (2016) *What is populism?* Philadelphia, PA: University of Philadelphia Press.

Nguyen, C. (2017) Labour market insecurity and generalized trust in welfare state context. *European Sociological Review*, 33(2): 225–39.

Niskanen, W. (1971) *Bureaucracy and representative government.* New York, NY: Aldine-Atherton.

OECD (Organisation for Economic Co-operation and Development) (1981) *The welfare state in crisis.* Paris: OECD.

Offe, C. (1984) *The contradictions of the welfare state.* London: Hutchinson.

Peters, B.G. (2015) *Advanced introduction to public policy.* Cheltenham: Edward Elgar.

Pierson, P. (2001) Coping with permanent austerity: welfare state restructuring in affluent democracies. In P. Pierson (ed) *The new politics of the welfare state.* Oxford: Oxford University Press.

Rawls, J. (1971) *A theory of justice.* Cambridge: Cambridge University Press.

Reeskens, T. and van Oorschot, W. (2013) Equity, equality, or need? A study of popular preferences for welfare redistribution principles across 24 European countries. *Journal of European Public Policy*, 20(8): 1174–95.

Rehm, P. (2011) Social policy by popular demand. *World Politics*, 63(2): 271–99.

Rehm, P., Hacker, J. and Schlesinger, M. (2012) Insecure alliances: risk, inequality and support for the welfare state. *American Political Science*, 106(2): 386–406.

Rodrik, D. (2014) When ideas trump interest: preferences, worldviews, and policy innovations. *Journal of Economic Perspectives*, 28(1): 189–208.

Rodrik, D. (2017) Populism and the economics of globalization. Available at: https://drodrik.scholar.harvard.edu/files/dani-rodrik/files/populism_and_the_economics_of_globalization.pdf (accessed 9 January 2018).

Romano, S. (2018) *Moralising poverty: The 'undeserving' poor in the public gaze.* Oxon: Routledge.

Rooduijn, M. (2014) The nucleus of populism: in search of the lowest common denominator. *Government and Opposition*, 49(4): 572–98.

Rooduijn, M. and Pauwels, T. (2011) Measuring populism: comparing two methods of content analysis. *West European Politics*, 34(6): 1272–83.

Rooduijn, M., Lange, S. and Brug, W. (2014) A populist zeitgeist? Programmatic contagion by populist parties in Western Europe. *Party Politics*, 20(4): 563–75.

Roosma, F. and van Oorschot, W. (2017) The social legitimacy of welfare states in European regions and countries: balancing between popular preferences and evaluations. In P. Kennet and N. Lendvai-Batton (eds) *Handbook of European social policy*. Oxon: Routledge.

Roosma, F., Gelisssen, J. and van Oorschot, W. (2012) The multidimensionality of welfare state attitudes: a European cross-national study. *Social Indicators Research*, 133: 235–55.

Roosma, F., van Oorschot, W. and Gelissen, J. (2014) The preferred role and perceived performance of the welfare state: European welfare attitudes from a multidimensional perspective. *Social Science Research*, 44: 200–10.

Roosma, F., van Oorschot, W. and Gelissen, J. (2016) The Achilles' heel of welfare state legitimacy: perception of overuse and underuse of social benefits in Europe. *Journal of European Public Policy*, 23(2): 177–96.

Schumacher, G. and Kersbergen, K. (2016) Do mainstream parties adapt to the welfare chauvinism of populist parties? *Party Politics*, 22(3): 300–12.

Starke, P. (2006) The politics of welfare state retrenchment: a literature review. *Social Policy & Administration*, 40(1): 104–20.

Svallfors, S. (2014) Welfare attitudes in context. In S. Svallfors (ed) *Welfare attitudes and beyond*. Stanford, CA: Stanford University Press.

Taylor-Gooby, P. (2017) Re-doubling the crises of the welfare state. *Journal of Social Policy*, 46(4): 815–35.

Taylor-Gooby, P. and Leruth, B. (ed) (2018) *Attitudes, aspirations and welfare. Social policy directions in uncertain times*. Cham: Palgrave Macmillan.

Taylor-Gooby, P., Leruth, B. and Chung, H, (2017) *After austerity – Welfare state transformation in Europe after the Great Recession*. Oxford: Oxford University Press.

Taylor-Gooby, P., Chung, H. and Leruth, B. (2018) The contribution of deliberative forums to studying welfare state attitudes. *Social Policy & Administration*, 52(4): 914–27.

Vandoninck, J., Meeusen, C. and Dejaeghere, Y. (2018) The relation between ethnic and civic views on citizenship: attitudes towards immigrants and sympathy for welfare recipients. *Social Policy & Administration*, 52(1): 158–71.

van Oorschot, W. (2006) Making the difference in social Europe: deservingness perceptions among citizens of European Welfare States. *Journal of European Social Policy*, 16(1): 23–42.

van Oorschot, W. and Roosma, F. (2015) The social legitimacy of differently targeted benefits. Discussion Paper No. 15/11, Improve, Working Papers.

van Oorschot, W., Roosma, F., Meuleman, B. and Reeskens, T. (eds) (2017) *The social legitimacy of targeted welfare: Attitudes to welfare deservingness*. Cheltenham: Edward Elgar.

Waal, J., Koster, W. and van Oorschot, W. (2013) Three worlds of welfare chauvinism? How welfare regimes affect support for distributing welfare to immigrants in Europe. *Journal of Comparative Policy Analysis: Research and Practice*, 15(2): 164–81.

3

Why inequality matters

Introduction

We have seen an increase in inequality in many countries over the last 15 to 20 years. This chapter focuses on why inequality matters for welfare states, why we should have an interest in this topic and how this is related to issues of populism and welfare chauvinism. This is done by trying to systematise the knowledge we have on why inequality matters for, and in relation to, economic growth, for health and for social cohesion. It also discusses why trickle-down economics does not work. The development in inequality is analysed by showing the development using traditional aspects such as the Gini coefficient, but also reflecting on, and showing, data on inequality in health and how this can be seen as connected to change in economic inequality. Real-wage development is also included as a reason why there has been increasing inequality (see also the data presented in Chapter 5), combined with inequality in wealth and capital income. As such, even if people get a job (as is the focus of Chapter 4), this is not a guarantee that they will have a standard of living above the poverty line, so, in fact, being the working poor. Inequality is not just an issue related to the economic sphere of societal development, and therefore the last section points towards other types of inequality because inequality in the economic part of society also has implications for other spheres of society.

The chapter does not look into equality issues related to, for example, the hidden economy or the use of tax planning and/or tax havens to put money aside so that rich people have low taxation on income, or income from wealth that they do not pay any tax on. This is despite the fact that looking into inequalities in wealth will, presumably, indicate that the degree of inequality is higher than often depicted, and certainly also that the ability to both avoid and evade paying taxes will cause even higher inequalities in the years to come, unless an international agreement is made to close tax-evasion loopholes. To a more limited extent, the chapter also looks into the possible political reasons for the development, although only a few aspects are presented (for two types of political explanations, see Hopkin and Lynch, 2016).

The topic is important not only in itself, but also, as will be shown in Chapter 6, because the feeling of being left behind and 'others' getting a better economic position can be a reason for support for populist parties as they point to positions of 'them' and 'us'. This might vary across countries dependent on whether one, for example, sees a high level of income as something that the individual has deserved through effort and mobility (Roex et al, 2018).

A short depiction of the development

The change in equality and its possible consequences have come under increasing discussion in recent years (Stiglitz, 2012; Atkinson, 2014, 2015; Piketty, 2014; Reich, 2015); therefore, this section briefly describes the development. The issue of the possible negative consequences of inequality have been discussed not only in academic circles, but also among world business leaders at their meeting in Davos in January 2017 (Dorling, 2018), and again in 2018. In several countries, interventions after the financial crisis to reduce benefits to certain groups (see Chapter 5) and to give tax cuts, in particular, to higher-income groups caused increased inequality. Typically, as in the UK, this took the form of the unemployed, lone parents and larger families being the losers, and dual-earner families and those with higher incomes (often in their 50s and 60s) being the winners (Agostini et al, 2017). The fact that there have been losers from the intervention, despite not in general retrenchment terms, indicates that the interventions, as shown later, caused increased inequality (for general descriptions, see also Klein, 2017; Varoufakis, 2017).

This section gives a short depiction of the development in economic inequality over the last 10 to 15 years, although inequality has been on the rise over a longer time perspective (Brys et al, 2016). It uses the most common metric for economic inequality, the Gini coefficient, after the impact of public transfers and taxes and duties, as the central way of showing the development. As with all statistics, it can be criticised for not being precise enough, as well as the fact that there might be many issues at stake, such as the hidden economy, the individual/family, generational position (students, pensioners) and so on (for an overview, see Greve, 2015). However, for an analysis over time, these issues are less important, unless, for example, there has been strong change in some of these aspects, which does not seem to be the case. Thus, using the same indicator over time will give an impression of the situation and how it has developed, including whether there are differences among welfare states from different regimes. This is shown in Table 3.1.

The surprising picture in the table is that inequality has increased a lot in the northern welfare states, France and Spain, and has been reduced in liberal and Eastern Europe. However, this does not follow the classical descriptions of welfare state development. These data (as do part of the data in Chapter 5) point to the differences among countries being less strong than they used to be, as the coefficient of variation falls during the time period in question. This is despite the fact that welfare state intervention is often seen as better able to reduce poverty and inequality in the more high-spending universalistic welfare states (Saltkjel and Malmberg-Heimonen, 2017).

There has also been an increase in many countries as to how much the richest 1% earn (Piketty, 2014). Looking into the development since 1981 (until around 2012), it has, for example, doubled in the US and the UK, but also 'increased by 70% and now reach about 7–8% in Finland, Norway and Sweden which have traditionally been characterized by a more equal income distribution' (Brys et al, 2016: 7). In Appendix 3.1, the development for the richest 1% in selected countries is shown. Thus, not only has inequality been on the rise, but what the richest get has also caused an overall increase in the difference

Table 3.1: Development in Gini coefficient since 2006 for the EU28 and selected European Union member states, and change during the period

GEO/TIME	2006	2008	2010	2012	2014	2016	2017	Change 2006– 2017
EU28	–	–	30.5	30.5	31.0	30.8	–	0.3
Czech Republic	25.3	24.7	24.9	24.9	25.1	25.1	24.5	–0.8
Denmark	23.7	25.1	26.9	26.5	27.7	27.7	27.6	3.9
Germany	26.8	30.2	29.3	28.3	30.7	29.5	–	2.7
Ireland	31.9	29.9	30.7	30.5	31.1	29.5	–	–2.4
Spain	31.9	32.4	33.5	34.2	34.7	34.5	34.1	2.2
France	27.3	29.8	29.8	30.5	29.2	29.3	–	2.0
Italy	32.1	31.2	31.7	32.4	32.4	33.1	–	1.0
Poland	33.3	32.0	31.1	30.9	30.8	29.8	29.2	–4.1
Sweden	24.0	25.1	25.5	26.0	26.9	27.6	–	3.6
UK	32.5	33.9	32.9	31.3	31.6	31.5	–	–1.0

Note: If all years are not available, the available year is used to calculate the change from 2006 to 2016.

Source: EUROSTAT, European Union Statistics on Income and Living Conditions (EU-SILC) survey (ilc_di120), accessed 15 August 2018

between low- and high-income earners, partly also reflecting a change in capital income.

A change in capital income due to an increase in the difference in wealth among citizens helps in explaining part of the reason for increased inequality. This is because within the Organisation for Economic Co-operation and Development (OECD) area, the 10% with the highest wealth hold around 50% of all wealth, while it is 25% of all income (OECD, 2016). Including tax avoidance and evasion, which is higher among the wealthy, would further increase the development in inequality (Alstadsæter et al, 2017) as the income and wealth from this is often not part of official statistics. Still, tax expenditures also play a role for the level of inequality as they 'are more beneficial to middle and higher income groups' (Avram, 2018: 284), and this is further part of the hidden welfare state. These two elements also point to the fact that an effective and progressive tax system might be able to reduce inequalities; therefore, a reduction in taxes will mainly cause increased inequality, especially as the trickle-down economy does not work (see later). Wealth also causes racial divisions as part of the continued wealth inequality is due to inheritance and the ability to save, for example, in the US, white households have ten times more wealth than black or Latino families (Williams, 2017).

The relation between inequality and societal development

The development in economic inequality has often been discussed as a separate topic, although with analyses looking into aspects such as changes in welfare state spending and the impact of taxes and duties on the level of inequality. Business cycles and change in the relation between workers' and capital's share of economic development have also been an issue. Here, the focus is, first, on the possible link between inequality and social mobility, before embarking on the broader agenda of the possible impact of other types of approaches. Economic inequality has also been argued to be one reason for support for populism, although it is presumably so that this is not the only factor explaining the rise in support (Inglehart and Norris, 2016).

High levels of economic inequality also risk lowering social mobility as some might not dare to invest in human capital, or have the support to do so, and there is more social mobility in equal societies (Cingano, 2014). This might have an impact on economic growth (see also later). If people do not invest in themselves, or the welfare state does not support education, then this increases the likelihood that the intergenerational improvement of social mobility is reduced, thus causing a so-called negative social inheritance.

Therefore, policies to combat economic inequality might have an impact not only on economic inequality directly, but also on the level of social mobility in a longer-term perspective. This is because further education seems to be one of the possible options to reduce the level of inequality (Kamat, 2016). Even accepting the importance of education, the already-existing inequality in the level of education therefore causes inequalities in income, job options, political influence and the possibility of children getting an education (Robertson, 2016). Mobility research clearly shows a relation between origin, education and destination (Payne, 2017), and therefore inequality at the starting point for individuals will, for some, influence mobility in societies, including a risk of lower educational attainment than could otherwise be achieved.

From other studies (Wilkinson and Picket, 2009; Picket and Wilkinson, 2015), we further know that economic inequality negatively influences issues such as obesity, crime, teenage births and higher health-care costs; thus, a rising or constant high level of inequality can have negative repercussions on societies' ability to prosper. Furthermore, issues such as anxiety, stress and general well-being can also be influenced by the level of inequality (Wilkinson and Picket, 2018). This development has taken place despite increased emphasis in the European Union (EU) on the possible positive impact of looking at social investment policies.

In general, people with high wealth are more likely to have better health than others. The same picture is found when looking at income. People with higher incomes also have better health, and those who find it difficult to manage their economic situation and pay their bills also have a lower quality of life than others (see also later). The relation between well-being, happiness and inequality also points in this direction. Therefore, when people feel that their position in society is at risk of being less favourable than it used to be, this opens the possibility for support for populist politics and parties.

There can even be a correlation between economic inequality and rising health-care costs. There is evidence that economic inequality impacts health and social issues not only in the most unequal societies, but also in the Nordic welfare states. In other words, increasing economic inequality will also lead to increased health-care costs due to the need for increased contact with doctors, more hospitalisation, generally poorer health and early deaths, and also reduced social cohesion. An American study argues that increased inequality affects mortality as much as by three to five years from first experiencing it (Picket and Wilkinson, 2015).

There are policies available to tackle this inequality, including public sector spending, as well as taxes and duties. There is still an impact from these, meaning that inequality would have been higher without the interventions. Still, it is possible to design taxes to reduce inequality, and enhance growth (Brys et al, 2016), using a variety of measures, including broadening the tax base, the use of progressive taxes (and not only on personal income) and so on.

Inequality and growth: why trickle-down does not work

A central argument for why increasing inequality is not a problem has been that when and if a society grows richer through economic growth, those with a low income will also have an increase in their income – that a rising tide, as historically argued by John F. Kennedy, would rise all boats,[1] and not only the yachts. It is further often argued that this will be the case because increasing inequality will, over time, increase the likelihood of getting a job. A prime reason for this is that rising inequality, often in the wake of tax cuts for those with the highest income, will cause higher economic growth. Higher economic growth would make it possible for more people to get a job or a better job than before. Trickle-down economics, as well as the Laffer curve, can also be considered part of what has been labelled narrative economics (Shiller, 2017). Trickle-down was popular in the early 1930s in the US and then the 'theory lost persuasive narrative' (Shiller, 2017: 22). Narratives can be truth, but they can also be wishful thinking, and they might have a strong impact on voters' perceptions, and thereby be part of why populism can gain ground.

There are several difficult issues at stake here. One argument is whether, in fact, there will be higher economic growth as a consequence of the increase in inequality. More broadly, there seems to be agreement with the fact that:

> inequality can undermine progress in health and education, cause investment-reducing political and economic instability, and undercut the social consensus required to adjust in the face of major shocks, and, thus … it tends to reduce the pace and durability of growth. (Ostry et al, 2014: 5)

Ostry et al (2014) reference several other published articles and reports, and their argument is in line with a 2014 report from the OECD, which states that 'the econometric analysis suggests that income inequality has a negative and statistically significant impact on subsequent growth' (Cingano, 2014: 6), going on to argue that based on a 25-year time period, 'a 1 Gini point reduction in inequality would raise average growth by slightly more than 0.1 points percentage points per year' (Cingano, 2014: 18). In the short term, it is even argued that there is variation across countries, so that in countries with large inequalities, the impact in general is larger. One of the reasons for the negative impact is that high levels of inequalities reduce the willingness to invest in human capital. Another possible reason is that people with high incomes spend less as a proportion of their income than lower-income households, and, therefore, a change in inequality can reduce the overall level of demand, and might also reduce the automatic stabilisers from public financing. Lastly, there is the possibility that the willingness to take risks is reduced because there is only limited support in the less generous welfare states for those who are unsuccessful.

At the same time, however, it is a strong argument as to why it is not sufficient to give incentives by tax reductions, which will increase inequality, and then hope that those with low or no income would gain by the increasing inequality. Furthermore, it indicates that rising inequality is not only an issue in relation to social cohesion; rather, it can, in fact, have negative repercussions on overall economic development. Therefore, in contrast to policies that increase inequality, an approach towards a higher degree of equality could be growth enhancing.

At the same time, as described in classical economics, taxation can ensure that negative externalities, for example, from pollution, can be reduced. Also, using taxes to reduce economic inequality makes it possible to be able to make, for example, social investments, which might make it possible to invest in human capital and/or more welfare in different societies over a longer time perspective. The reduction in taxation on companies and higher incomes in recent years has implicitly implied higher levels of inequality. Given the high degree of inequality of wealth and increasing globalisation, this might be a field where further international cooperation is needed (Piketty, 2017). There can thus be a trade-off between inequality and well-being in a broader understanding.

A possible reason for trickle-down still being argued and pursued in tax reforms in different countries might be due to the fact that 'the rise in inequality can in many cases be traced directly or indirectly to changes in the balance of power' (Atkinson, 2015: 82). Thus, the balance of power can, unsurprisingly, influence what is decided; however, at the same time, many of those losing out due to tax 'reforms' support this development in the hope of, especially, getting a job. Therefore, an idea or normative position that tax cuts increase jobs might be supported by voters even when they risk losing welfare benefits or services as they believe that they will gain at a later stage. The difference in perceptions of the impact of inequality (Alesina et al, 2004) might also be of importance for voters' viewpoints related to trickle-down. Positions on inequality can also be embedded in relation to viewpoints on intergenerational redistribution, and thus an understanding that those in old age are worse off might help in understanding policies to support the elderly, including a higher degree of deservingness. This can, at least, be witnessed among young adults in the US (Prinzen, 2017).

Non-monetary inequality

As discussed earlier in this chapter, most of the time, inequality has been an issue related to the intended and unintended outcomes of policy interventions, including replacement rates and welfare state spending (as will be depicted in Chapter 5). However, there has gradually been an increased focus not only on the possible causality from change in the economic system and economic policy, but also the possible causality from change in economic inequality and other aspects of societies' development – ranging from teenage births to crime – with Wilkinson and Picket's book from 2009, and also the latest from 2018, setting a new agenda for the possible impact of economic inequality (Wilkinson and Picket, 2009, 2018).

A possible issue is inequality in opportunities, and the lack of opportunities might be a reason why people search for other solutions (as returned to in Chapter 6). Overall, it seems that with growing inequality come differences in the degree of opportunities. This includes the consequence of a lack of social capital, where families with larger social capital can better support their children, such as in education (Halpern, 2005). Halpern also points to several other areas where lack of social capital can influence development, such as health, crime and so on. It is difficult to measure opportunities and, to a greater extent, related inequalities (Ferreira and Peragine, 2015); despite this, one needs to be aware of the possible impact on perceptions of and support for welfare state development. If people feel that their opportunities are reduced, rightly or wrongly, due to migration or globalisation, then this may possibly lead to looking for and voting for persons/parties who will do something about it, including populist suggestions to reduce migration and provide stronger support for national citizens.

Whether inequalities in opportunities influence economic growth can be debated; however, it cannot be rejected that there is a connection as there is 'some suggestive evidence of a negative association between overall income inequality and subsequent growth' (Ferreira et al, 2014: 18), even though the calculation is not statistically significant. This is partly due to the fact that if inequality is high, some people do not pursue education, especially if there are fees.

There has long been knowledge that there is a relation between income and happiness, at least until a certain level is reached. This holds across nations as well as within nations. However, it is the case that a continued growth in income does not necessarily cause a higher level of happiness (Easterlin, 1995, 2001). This can also be seen as an argument that after a certain level of income, further increases will not increase well-being, and thus higher economic inequality will not increase happiness. Therefore, one can also ask the question: 'How much is enough?' (Skidelsky and Skidelsky, 2013). Finally, unhappy people are not as productive as happy people; therefore, trying to support well-being can also imply better productivity.

It is not only income, but also the types and quality of jobs, that influence happiness. Given that good-quality jobs are often highly paid, this gives a double impact: not only influencing happiness, but also engagement, loneliness, security and so on (Dorling, 2010).

The fact that there are many other types of inequality can also be witnessed in an OECD (2017) study. There are differences in educational attainment levels, higher unemployment for young people and lower income and less good health for migrants. As argued in the report, it is the case that 'Inequalities also shape the way people feel about themselves and how they relate to society: they can undermine people's sense of self-worth and aspiration, leading – particularly among young people – to resignation, mental health problems and anti-social behavior' (OECD, 2017: 66). It has also been argued that large inequalities in well-being persist. Especially problematic from a long-term perspective is that as the better-off have better health, better access to training and children who do better with regard to education (OECD, 2016), this points to the fact that existing divides will continue and, given the possible changes in the labour market (see Chapter 4), might even be aggravated in the future. Further, inequality in well-being can reduce trust in the government's ability to help and creates social barriers. Even when looking into non-monetary issues, the differences among countries, to a large degree, follow the division in relation to monetary indicators, so that the highest degree of equality in Europe can be found in the Nordic countries (OECD, 2017); at the same time, the OECD (2017) report shows that there is a correlation between income and life satisfaction.

Inequality in health has long been documented, including that the division within short geographical distances can be very large, such as seven years along the Jubilee line in London. In Stockton-on-Tees, the difference in life expectancy between different areas is 17 years for men and 11 years for women (Bambra, 2016), making it easy to understand a critique from those with shorter life expectancy and a lower standard of living of what they might perceive as the elite.

Overall, this implies that with growing monetary inequality, there will also be growing inequality in non-monetary factors in societies. This can further be the case because high levels of social trust reduce the risk of crime, increase civic engagement and even increase economic growth (Brewer et al, 2014).

Inequality and welfare chauvinism

The possible link between inequality and welfare chauvinism can obviously be related to the fact that if some groups see and have the feeling that others are getting increases in their standard of living but their own prospect of getting a job (see Chapter 4) or an increase in real wages (see Chapter 3) is diminishing, then they will try to find someone to blame. The prospects for their children might also not look so good (see more in Chapter 6). It is argued that one of the possible consequences of growing inequality is that 'citizens can lose confidence in institutions, eroding social cohesion and confidence in the future' (Dabla-Norris et al, 2015: 6).

This blame can be based on clear information and knowledge, but it can also be part of a feeling that someone needs to be blamed for the fact that their own position has been weakened, as many in the middle classes in a number of countries have felt over time. This blame may be directed not only at those who have gained high incomes (such as the 1%), but also at those who are seen by some as putting pressure on the availability of jobs and income, such as migrants – and this does not necessarily depend on whether this is just imagined or is factually correct (see more in Chapter 6).

Some have even argued that 'one alternative to high inequality is fascism. When people are very unhappy, they can be more easily persuaded to vote for far-right parties' (Dorling, 2018: 98). Thus, inequality, not only in relation to economic issues, but also in other spheres of life, such as happiness and opportunities, might change voters' perception of what the right future development for a society is. Blaming others is thus a possible consequence of changes in inequality and structural change in societies (see also Chapter 4).

Social polarisation as a consequence of increases in inequality can lead to populism (Anselmi, 2018), although naturally in varying degrees. This is also due to the fact that 'people feel generous or altruistic toward the poor only if they have a sense of belonging or shared identity with them' (Alt and Iversen, 2017: 23), and also that less segmentation in society increases support for redistribution. Therefore, the implication of an increase in inequality (as shown earlier in the chapter) is that some will be in favour of having welfare policies towards native citizens as a consequence of less cohesive societies.

In principle, stronger inequality would be expected to cause, at the outset, a stronger demand for policies causing more redistribution, at least by the less affluent. This can, however, be in conflict with the fact that with growing prosperity, there can be less demand for redistribution as there might be 'a tradeoff between egalitarian policies and economic development, with the latter growing in importance over time' (VanHeuvelen, 2017: 60). A caveat is that the latest data are from 2010, and thus the consequences of the financial crisis are not included in the study. Furthermore, the less affluent might worry that benefits will also be paid to some who they do not see as in need. This also reflects changes in conditionality issues (Watts and Fitzpatrick, 2018), including political attempts to reduce access to benefits for non-national citizens (Shutes, 2016) as a way of gaining support for changes to and the legitimacy of the welfare state. Finally, some groups have historically been able to cope by having a job, and they would prefer this instead of benefits (see also Chapters 4 and 6).

Conclusion

Inequality can have dire consequence for societies' development, including reduced social cohesion. As even argued by Reich (2015), to save capitalism, it is important that societies do something about growing inequalities in societies so that all feel that they are part of society and not strangers in their own country (as returned to Chapter 6). The increase in inequality in recent years across most welfare states, with a higher proportion of income and wealth going to the richest in many countries, forms a natural background and reason for support for populist parties arguing against the elite – even if the support does not necessarily lead to more equality-driven policies. This is the case as the elite are those who have gained by the increased level of inequality.

Note

[1] See: www.jfklibrary.org/JFK/JFK-in-History/JFK-on-the-Economy-and-Taxes.aspx (accessed 20 December 2017).

References

Agostini, P., Hills, J. and Sutherland, H. (2017) Were we really all in it together? The distributional impact of the 2010–15 UK Coalition government's tax–benefit policy changes. *Social Policy & Administration*, early view.

Alesina, A., Di Tella, R. and MacCuloch, R. (2004) Inequality and happiness: are Europeans and Americans different? *Journal of Public Economics*, 88: 2009–42.

Alstadsæter, A., Johannesen, N. and Zucman, G. (2017) Tax evasion and inequality. Available at: http://gabriel-zucman.eu/leaks

Alt, J. and Iversen, T. (2017) Inequality, labor market segmentation, and preferences for redistribution. *American Journal of Political Science*, 61(1): 21–36.

Anselmi, M. (2018) *Populism: An introduction*. Oxon: Routledge.

Atkinson, A.B. (2014) After Piketty. *British Journal of Sociology*, 65(4): 619–38.

Atkinson, A.B. (2015) *Inequality: What can be done*. Cambridge: Harvard University Press.

Avram, S. (2018) Who benefits from the 'hidden welfare state'? The distributional effects of personal income tax expenditures in six countries. *Journal of European Social Policy*, 28(3): 271–93.

Bambra, C. (2016) *Health divides: Where you live can kill you*. Bristol: Policy Press.

Brewer, K., Oh, H. and Sharma, S. (2014) 'Crowding in' or 'crowding out'? An examination of the impact of the welfare state on generalized social trust. *International Journal of Social Welfare*, 23(1): 61–8.

Brys, B., Perret, S., Thomas, A. and O'Reilly, P. (2016) *Tax design for inclusive economic growth*. OECD Taxation Working Papers, No. 26, Paris: OECD.

Cingano, F. (2014) *Trends in income inequality and its impact on economic growth*. OECD Social, Employment and Migration Working Papers No. 163, Paris: OECD.

Dabla-Norris, E., Kochhar, K., Suphaphiphat, N., Ricka, F. and Tsounta, E. (2015) Causes and consequences of income inequality: a global perspective. IMF Staff Discussion Note, SDN/15/13, IMF.

Dorling, D. (2010) *Injustices: Why social inequality persists.* Bristol: Policy Press.

Dorling, D. (2018) *Do we need economic inequality?* Cambridge: Polity.

Easterlin, R.A. (1995) Will raising the income of all increase the happiness of all? *Journal of Economic Behavior and Organization*, 27: 35–47.

Easterlin, R.A. (2001) Income and happiness: towards a unified theory. *The Economic Journal*, 11: 465–84.

Ferreira, F. and Peragine, V. (2015) Equality of opportunity: theory and evidence. IZA Discussion Paper No. 8994, IZA.

Ferreira, F.H.G., Lakner, C., Lugo, M.A. and Ozler, B. (2014) Inequality of opportunity and economic growth: a cross-country analysis. Policy Research Working Paper 6915, World Bank.

Greve, B. (2015) *Welfare and the welfare state: Present and future.* Oxon: Routledge.

Halpern, D. (2005) *Social capital.* Cambridge: Polity.

Hopkin, J. and Lynch, J. (2016) Winner-take-all politics in Europe? European inequality in comparative perspective. *Politics and Society*, 44(3): 335–43.

Inglehart, R. and Norris, P. (2016) Trump, Brexit, and the rise of populism: economic have-nots and cultural backlash. HKS Faculty Research Working Paper Series, RWP16-026.

Kamat, S. (2016) Education's relevance for Piketty. *British Journal of Sociology of Education*, 37(6): 873–8.

Klein, N. (2017) *No is not enough: Defeating the new shock politics.* St. Ives: Allen Lane.

OECD (Organisation for Economic Co-operation and Development) (2016) *The productivity–inclusiveness nexus.* Paris: OECD.

OECD (2017) *How's life? 2017: Measuring well-being.* Paris: OECD.

Ostry, J., Berg, A. and Tsangarides, C. (2014) Redistribution, inequality and growth. IMF Staff Discussion Note, SDN/14/02.

Payne, G. (2017) *The new social mobility: How the politicians got it wrong.* Bristol: Policy Press.

Picket, K. and Wilkinson, R. (2015) Income inequality and health: a causal review. *Social Science and Medicine*, 128: 316–26.

Piketty, T. (2014) *Capital in the twenty-first century.* Cambridge: The Belknap Press of Harvard University Press.

Piketty, T.H. (2017) *Chronicles on our troubled times.* Milton Keynes: Penguin.

Prinzen, K. (2017) The moral economy of intergenerational redistribution in an ageing society: a qualitative analysis of young adults' beliefs in the United States. *Social Policy & Administration*, 51(7): 1267–86.

Reich, R. (2015) *Saving capitalism: For the many, not the few*. New York, NY: Alfred A. Knopf.

Robertson, S. (2016) Piketty, capital and education: a solution to, or problem in, rising social inequalities? *British Journal of Sociology of Education*, 37(6): 823–35.

Roex, K., Huijts, T. and Sieben, I. (2018) Attitudes towards income inequality: 'winners' versus 'losers' of the perceived meritocracy. *Acta Sociologica*, pp 1–21, DOI: 10.117/0001699317748340.

Saltkjel, T. and Malmberg-Heimonen, I. (2017) Welfare generosity in Europe: a multi-level study of material deprivation and income poverty among disadvantaged groups. *Social Policy & Administration*, 51(7): 1287–310.

Shiller, R. (2017) Narrative economics. Cowles Foundation Discussion Paper No. 2069, Yale University. Available at: https://cowles.yale.edu/sites/default/files/files/pub/d20/d2069.pdf

Shutes, I. (2016) Work-related conditionality and the access to social benefits of national citizens, EU and non-EU Citizens. *Journal of Social Policy*, 45(4): 691–707.

Skidelsky, R. and Skidelsky, E. (2013) *How much is enough? Money and the good life*. London: Penguin.

Stiglitz, J. (2012) *The price of inequality*. London: W.W. Norton & Company.

VanHeuvelen, T (2017) Unequal views on inequality: cross-national support for redistribution 1985–2011. *Social Science Research*, 64: 43–66.

Varoufakis, Y. (2017) *And the weak suffer what they must? Europe, austerity and the threat to global stability*. London: Vintage.

Watts, B. and Fitzpatric, S. (2018) *Welfare conditionality*. Oxon: Routledge.

Wilkinson, R. and Pickett, K. (2009) *The spirit level: Why greater equality makes societies stronger*. London: Bloomsbury Press.

Wilkinson, R. and Pickett, K. (2018) *The inner level: How more equal societies reduce stress, restore sanity and improve everyone's well-being*. St. Ives: Allen Lane.

Williams, R. (2017) *The privileges of wealth: Rising inequality and the growing racial divide*. Oxon: Routledge.

Appendix 3.1: Development in the share of income for the richest 1% since 1980

Year	Denmark	Sweden	Germany	France	Italy	Spain	Czech Republic	Poland	UK	Ireland	USA
1980	0.054718	0.0413	0.106479	0.081749	0.069		0.025806				0.10671
1981	0.053768	0.0407		0.08214	0.0647	0.07628				0.0536	0.11052
1982	0.052137	0.0408		0.075166	0.064	0.07953				0.0579	0.11264
1983	0.052704	0.0445	0.098379	0.073301	0.0634	0.07792		0.041996		0.0594	0.11514
1984	0.052644	0.0436		0.074687	0.0654	0.07812		0.047299		0.0547	0.12496
1985	0.052123	0.0459		0.077374	0.0681	0.08119	0.025377	0.041544		0.0528	0.12553
1986	0.051506	0.0449	0.102151	0.08247	0.0713	0.08878		0.041509		0.0517	0.12209
1987	0.052447	0.0473		0.090191	0.0745	0.09152		0.042874		0.0517	0.13307
1988	0.051779	0.0508		0.09155	0.076	0.09186	0.029903	0.041377		0.0518	0.14876
1989	0.052362	0.0545	0.114403	0.0952	0.0779	0.0901		0.044037		0.0537	0.14465
1990	0.051699	0.052		0.093316	0.0778	0.08803			0.098005	0.0559	0.14542
1991	0.050115	0.0695		0.091472	0.0784	0.08469			0.103208	0.0614	0.13891
1992	0.050155	0.0584	0.094877	0.086162	0.0781	0.08422	0.06537	0.076384	0.098601	0.0659	0.15013
1993	0.051312	0.0593		0.090859	0.0792	0.08219	0.06932	0.08435	0.103608	0.0636	0.14644
1994	0.050038	0.0718		0.091786	0.0799	0.08271	0.073345	0.098926	0.106254	0.0668	0.14687
1995	0.050348	0.06	0.081567	0.092259	0.08134	0.08287	0.077448	0.109643	0.107423	0.0704	0.15283
1996	0.051198	0.0699		0.100334		0.08286	0.081629	0.094024	0.119008	0.0713	0.15967
1997	0.052441	0.0761		0.104378		0.08431	0.081681	0.102669	0.120706	0.0766	0.16629
1998	0.054004	0.0817	0.118241	0.106739	0.0874	0.08844	0.081731	0.110382	0.125299	0.0877	0.16923

(continued)

Year	Denmark	Sweden	Germany	France	Italy	Spain	Czech Republic	Poland	UK	Ireland	USA
1999	0.054728	0.093		0.106016	0.0882	0.09345	0.08178	0.104433	0.13239	0.0893	0.17709
2000	0.057301	0.1112		0.110256	0.0909	0.09749	0.081827	0.104415	0.135087	0.0966	0.18266
2001	0.056241	0.0862	0.11404	0.113187	0.0928	0.09632	0.081874	0.109246	0.133862	0.0935	0.17268
2002	0.055454	0.0759	0.110506	0.109487	0.0928	0.09322	0.081919	0.111651	0.130265	0.0924	0.17058
2003	0.055019	0.0762	0.105382	0.113522	0.0936	0.09914	0.084492	0.102893	0.132394	0.094	0.17202
2004	0.055657	0.0787	0.111034	0.116172	0.0928	0.10228	0.089132	0.119821	0.133006	0.0985	0.18322
2005	0.057812	0.0899	0.129334	0.11471	0.0935	0.11	0.094227	0.121301	0.142238	0.1046	0.19372
2006	0.059127	0.0953	0.132249	0.112355	0.09721	0.12741	0.086673	0.131678	0.148223	0.1131	0.201
2007	0.061202	0.099466	0.140358	0.116861	0.09861	0.11236	0.09098	0.133973	0.154418	0.106	0.19867
2008	0.060518	0.089896	0.145165	0.115699	0.09657	0.09827	0.113368	0.130787	0.154047	0.0968	0.1952
2009	0.054375	0.084126	0.131741	0.101755	0.09375	0.09298	0.10146	0.123063	0.15423	0.0963	0.18541
2010	0.064146	0.089838	0.131313	0.108437		0.08687	0.094298	0.119509	0.125482	0.0953	0.198
2011		0.090085	0.131135	0.114529		0.09034	0.094415	0.121144	0.129304	0.0937	0.196
2012		0.086674	0.130238	0.10432		0.08576	0.102016	0.122013	0.126969	0.0967	0.20779
2013		0.087267	0.132344	0.107946			0.091225	0.121006	0.145269	0.0979	0.19592
2014				0.107965			0.090934	0.128513	0.138827	0.0995	0.202
2015							0.091967	0.133416		0.115	

Source: https://wid.world/data/ (accessed 16 August 2018)

4

Dualisation and the labour market

Introduction

Having a job is central for an individual's standard of living, quality of life and feeling of being part of society. Dualisation in the labour market can thereby be a central issue having an impact on, and seemingly moving countries towards, increasingly split societies – especially as it might also negatively influence the ability to finance welfare states. Even more simply argued, the need for jobs for persons with different qualifications, including fewer jobs for low-skilled persons, can cause a strong reduction in people's trust in the future, both for themselves and their children. This can further influence the perception of what the state is able to do, and the state might even be blamed for the loss of jobs, despite the fact that, in reality, the state could not have influenced it. The increased divide in the labour market, and the related ability to be included in, or excluded from, society and access to different goods and services, might therefore be an explanation as to why populist parties have had the ability to gain support. Therefore, this chapter depicts, at an overall level, how and what the consequences for social cohesion have been of the developments in the labour market of recent years. It first includes a short description of possible future trends in the labour market and how they can influence welfare state developments. It further includes reference to the Europeanisation and globalisation discussion as this is also an issue in relation to labour market developments, including how this might have an impact on preferences for state intervention.

Technology and jobs

Throughout history, technology has had an impact on the number of jobs. In general, there are two interpretations of the impact of technology on jobs: a bright side and a dark side (Greve, 2017).[1] Historically, the argument has been that although new technology destroys jobs, new jobs will also be created. This is with reference to the movement from the countryside to cities, the Industrial Revolution and the coming of age of the use of new technology. The question is whether it is different this time (Mokyr et al, 2015). To put it another way, this time, will as many new jobs be created as the jobs that are wiped away by the use of new technology so that, overall, there will be the same number of jobs, or will there be fewer jobs? This is because, based on the classical article by Frey and Osborne (2013), it seems clear that 40–50% of the job functions we know today will be gone within 10–15 years. This might reduce the number of jobs by around 10%. Figure 4.1 shows the possible impact in a number of Organisation for Economic Co-operation and Development (OECD) countries.

The data in Figure 4.1 are a strong indicator that in all countries, there will be a substantial impact in the years to come. Countries still having a high number of industrial jobs will be even harder hit than other countries. In Europe, for example, the impact can thus be expected to be higher in Southern and Eastern Europe than in the Nordic and Central European countries. The implication of this is that technological change can cause divisions not only within each country, but also across Europe. Therefore, the legitimacy of, for example, the European Union (EU) can be influenced by this development as some might prefer to find a scapegoat outside one's own country. The EU, globalisation and migrants have seemingly been scapegoated in recent years.

Therefore, the question is not whether robots, information technology (IT) and artificial intelligence imply that many jobs will not exist in a few years' time, but whether and to what degree new jobs will be created. This is again not a sufficiently precise question to ask as even if new jobs are created, and naturally some will be, it is more important to ask who will get the new jobs. If jobs are destroyed, the feeling of loss might be very strong for those out of a job, and as we know by now, losing has a stronger impact on people than winning (Frey and Stutzer, 2002; Schwartz, 2004). Therefore, those losing their jobs can have a stronger negative attitude than those gaining a job, which increases overall discontent in society.

We also know that having a job is important for well-being (Easterlin, 2013). Therefore, losing one's job can have a strong negative impact on individuals' feelings (for an early argument, see Clark and Oswald, 1994). Unemployment has a negative impact on happiness (Frey and Stutzer, 2010). Involuntary unemployment, especially if it is the consequence of new technology, reduces happiness dramatically, not only due to economic reasons, but also due to the possible loss of social contact and self-esteem (Layard, 2005; Classen and Dunn, 2012).

The implication of this is that even if new jobs are created, the consequences for social cohesion can be strong as those losing their

Figure 4.1: The risk of automation in OECD countries

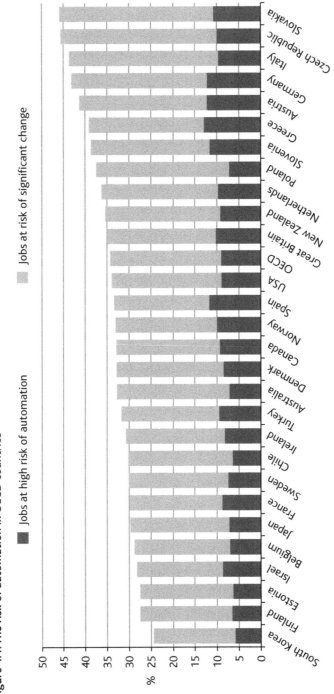

Source: OECD, Employment Outlook, 2017

job and having difficulties in re-entering the labour market, or perhaps never being able to enter again, will feel that loss very strongly. A central assumption of the argument that new jobs will be created is that new technology increases productivity, making goods cheaper, and that people will therefore have more buying power for new products, which leads to job creation as companies are then able to sell more goods and services. However, the increase in sales will only take place if those losing their job still have buying power; therefore, the impact of social benefits on the standard of living and the demand for goods and services in different welfare states becomes stronger. Welfare states with low replacement rates (see Chapter 5) thus have the risk that job losses will cause less demand, so that even cheaper goods might not be sold.

This further points to the fact that even if something at the overall general macro-level will be in balance, at least over time, this does not necessarily cause gains for all. This is because people on the margins of the labour market, who lose out from changes in societies, might turn to populist parties for the hope of a better day – and, as argued, losing is twice as negative as winning. Therefore, those parties holding out the hope to voters of new jobs can gain support.

One could perhaps argue that the ageing of the population will help in reducing the pressure on the labour market as more people will leave the labour market, with the risk of an increase in unemployment being possibly lower therefore than otherwise. However, this seems not to be case (Avent, 2017).

Dualisation: social inclusion or not

Central to development in recent years has been the question about dualisation in the labour market, including development towards more precarious working positions for many in the labour market as a consequence of new technology (Greve, 2017). This development has a variety of reasons, including that trade unions have less power today than previously (Palier and Thelen, 2010).

Dualisation can have different forms and be interpreted in a variety of ways. A possible three different forms can be understood by focusing on characteristics related to deepening, widening and new institutional dualism (Emmenegger et al, 2012). Dualisation can influence access to several benefits and not only jobs (for pensions, see Keune, 2018; for family-friendly working time, see Chung, 2018). Dualisation might also imply that those able to move away from routine jobs will have a stronger increase in wages (Cortes, 2016), which will then contribute to an increase in inequality.

In order to understand part of the reasons for the development, the overall depiction of the development in unemployment is first shown before looking into whether certain groups are at a higher risk of becoming unemployed depending on their educational attainment level. Table 4.1 shows the development in unemployment in the selected countries.

The impact of levels of education as a measure of where on the dualisation path individuals will be is illustrated by Table 4.2, which shows the unemployment rate for 20–64 year olds depending on the level of qualifications. Naturally, the level of unemployment has to be seen in light of the overall employment rate, which fell in most countries after the financial crisis. In several countries, it was only in 2017 that employment rates returned to the 2008 rate – some countries had a higher rate and some had a lower rate – indicating that the supply of labour is also strongly dependent on demand.

Table 4.1 is a clear indication not only that all countries were hit hard by the economic crisis, but also that some have recovered (especially in Eastern Europe, Germany and the UK) with lower unemployment rates than in 2008, although there are still high rates of unemployment in Southern Europe. In most countries, young people were harder hit as it reduced their options and possibilities of entering the labour market. In Figure 4.2 the situation in 2010 and 2017 for young people is shown.

Table 4.1: Unemployment rate of total active population in selected EU countries since 2008

GEO/TIME	2008	2010	2012	2014	2016	2017
EU28	7.0	9.6	10.5	10.2	8.6	7.7
Czech Republic	4.4	7.3	7.0	6.1	4.0	2.9
Denmark	3.4	7.5	7.5	6.6	6.2	5.7
Germany	7.4	7.0	5.4	5.0	4.1	3.8
Ireland	6.8	14.6	15.5	11.9	8.4	6.7
Spain	11.3	19.9	24.8	24.5	19.6	17.2
France	7.4	9.3	9.8	10.3	10.1	9.4
Italy	6.7	8.4	10.7	12.7	11.7	11.2
Poland	7.1	9.7	10.1	9.0	6.2	4.9
Sweden	6.2	8.6	8.0	7.9	6.9	6.7
UK	5.6	7.8	7.9	6.1	4.8	4.4

Source: EUROSTAT, une_rt_a (accessed 16 August 2018)

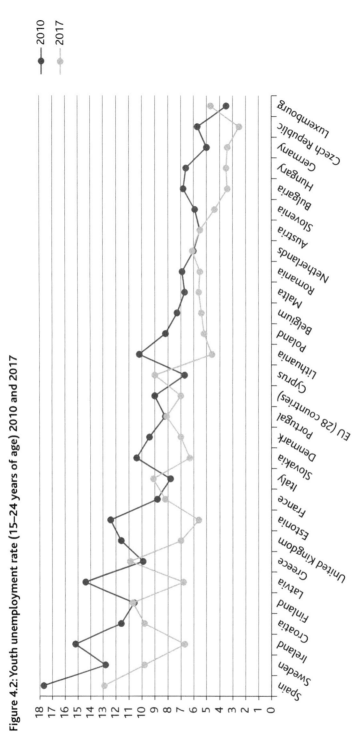

Figure 4.2: Youth unemployment rate (15–24 years of age) 2010 and 2017

Source: http://ec.europa.eu/eurostat/tgm/graph.do?tab=graph&plugin=1&pcode=tespm080&language=en&toolbox=data (accessed 16 August 2018)

Figure 4.2 is a clear indication of how high the unemployment rate has been for young people. Furthermore, in several countries, it would have been even higher if not for the tendency towards younger people participating in education. This shows a clear type of a divide in societies.

Thus, the financial crisis caused an increased divide in many countries, and thereby seemingly pushed those taking up jobs towards a possibly more negative stance. In some countries, this was argued to be due to the influx of migrant workers and/or refugees, thereby pushing some people towards a more nativist stance. This is related not only to age, but also to educational attainment level, especially as those hardest hit were those with the least education (see Table 4.2).

In all countries, those with lower levels of educational attainment have a higher unemployment rate than those with higher levels of education. Those with lower educational attainment levels were further hit harder by the economic changes in the wake of the last financial crisis. This indicates that a strong division in the labour market has taken place, and that, despite recovery, in several countries, those with low levels of qualifications who lost their jobs in 2017 still have a higher level of unemployment than before the crisis started. Furthermore, the picture between those with a higher and lower level of education is clear, pointing to a cleavage in support for globalisation and migration as well, with those that seemingly having less risk of

Table 4.2: Unemployment rate for 20–64 year olds in 2008 and 2017 dependent on educational attainment level in selected EU member states

	2008			2017		
	Levels			Levels		
GEO/TIME	0–2	3 and 4	5–8	0–2	3 and 4	5–8
EU28	10.7	6.3	3.8	14.7	6.7	4.6
Czech Republic	18.4	3.6	1.7	12.6	2.7	1.5
Denmark	4.3	2.7	2.3	7.6	4.5	4.8
Germany	16.7	7.3	3.4	9.9	3.3	2.0
Ireland	9.8	6.6	3.8	11.6	7.9	4.1
Spain	14.2	10.0	6.3	24.5	16.6	10.0
France	–	–	–	16.7	9.7	5.2
Italy	8.0	5.8	4.6	15.3	10.2	6.5
Poland	12.6	7.4	3.8	12.5	5.5	2.5
Sweden	8.4	4.9	3.5	16.2	5.0	4.1
UK	8.1	4.7	2.8	6.3	4.0	2.8

Note: Educational attainment level follows the International Standard Classification of Education (ISCED).

Source: Eurostat, une_educ_a (accessed 16 August 2018)

becoming unemployed as part of the development also being more open to migration. Naturally, the impact of immigration might be different depending on the time it takes place, with a study from 1991 to 2008 indicating that the increased supply of foreign refugee workers in Denmark had a positive impact for native unskilled workers (Foged and Peri, 2015).

Furthermore, in some countries, for those losing their jobs, there is a low level of compensation (see Chapter 5). For some, a declining level of unemployment benefit or a tightening of the conditions and lengths of unemployment benefit naturally makes them frustrated, which reduces their understanding and acceptance of the overall societal development, with some still having a good standard of living while theirs has been reduced, such as due to changes in conditionality (Watts and Fitzpatrick, 2018). Therefore, this adds to the risk that those on the margins of society with a reduced level of benefits and social protection in general will be persuaded by populist arguments promising solutions to what they perceive as the most pressing issue. The same issue arises for those employed in specific sectors at more risk due to technological development, as well as in regions in decline and with fewer job opportunities than in the areas of society with stronger and faster economic development.

Besides dualisation, it is also the case that labour markets are segmented, such as public–private, type of education, geographical position and so on. Therefore, they also have differences related to the need for qualifications, job security, the level of wages and so on. Emmenegger et al argue that the difference between the concepts of dualisation and segmentation includes the fact that polarisation does not necessarily focus on the politics of change. This is in contrast to dualisation, which 'implies that policies increasingly differentiate rights, entitlements, and services provided to different categories of recipients' (Emmenegger et al, 2012: 10). There are also many working in precarious types of jobs (see Figure 4.3).

There is diversity among countries in the number of people in precarious jobs but it has seemingly generally been on the rise. Dualisation can further vary over time and have a different impact depending on the social policy pursued in a country, and the development in recent years of the relocation of production as part of globalisation (see section later) has made the position in the labour market more precarious for many (Standing, 2011, 2014). Those in these more precarious positions will often have a higher risk of not being included in societal development, which might cause a risk of, and a demand for, a change in policies, including welfare state policies.

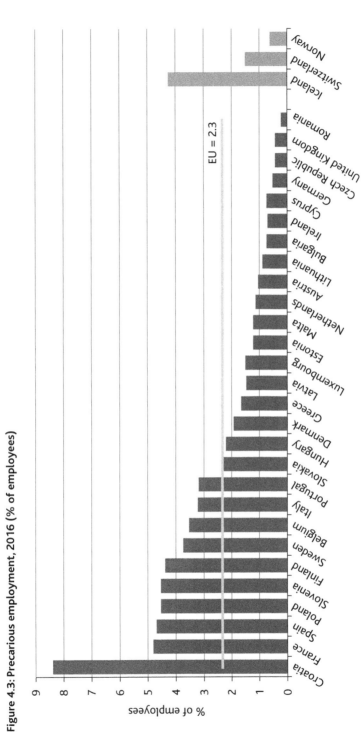

Figure 4.3: Precarious employment, 2016 (% of employees)

EU = 2.3

Source: ec.europa.eu/eurostat

In line with dualisation is job polarisation, which refers to the fact that there will be an expansion of the highest- and lowest-paid jobs compared to middle-wage jobs. Polarisation can be measured by considering the change in occupations of those with high, middle and low incomes. Overall, using data for 16 western countries in Europe between 1993 and 2010, based on employment codes, mean average wages and employment shares (with percentages of high-wage jobs being 31.7%, middle-wage jobs being 46.7% and low-wage jobs being 21.6%), the changes have been: high-paying occupations = +5.62; middle-paying occupations = −9.27; and low-paying occupations = +3.65 (Goos et al, 2014: 2512).

To put it another way, there have been increases in high- and low-paying jobs over time. Naturally, one can question the division into the three groups, and the data are also rather old; still, it is a clear indication of the changes in Western Europe. There is no indication that this divide and development has changed since then; thereby, an increasing part of the labour force might not be socially included in the sense that they have stable jobs with high enough pay not to make them the working poor. However, welfare service jobs (day-care, Long-Term Care (LTC) and primary education) might be less at risk of decreases in pay due to the need for personal interaction, and thereby less at risk of being replaced by the use of new technology.

A possible growing divide in the labour market as a consequence of dualisation and polarisation will cause an increased risk that societies will become more divided. Among other things, this is due to differences in access to different types of benefit in many welfare states, which is strongly connected to having a job, but also naturally as high-income groups are able to buy more goods and services than low-income households, who might be the working poor even if they have a job. This is because 'outsiders are defined as the (working) poor that would have to rely on modest (largely means-tested) public provision, primarily intended to ameliorate poverty' (Seeleib-Kaiser, 2013: 62). Thus, being an outsider influences access not only to jobs, but also to welfare and social policy benefits. To put it another way, a 'differentiating between social protection insiders and outsiders' (Seeleib-Kaiser, 2016: 222).

Naturally, there are divisions among countries due to institutional differences as to how dualisation influences employment security. Insecurity has risen as a consequence of the development, with a higher division of insecurity between insiders and outsiders in the corporatist countries (Chung, 2016). This insecurity can be expected to reduce social inclusion in society.

The precarious position of many, especially in new types of platform jobs (Hill, 2015), causes many more people to find that they are not really integrated into society; at the same time, they see that others have growing income (see the data on real wage development in Chapter 5). This increases understanding of the conflict as between 'them and us' and thereby support for populist parties and welfare chauvinism.

Even though precariousness has been on the agenda for some time, the definition of and ways of measuring it are not always clear. Eurostat, for example, used a definition of precariousness as 'meaning that the work contract did not exceed three months' duration',[2] which encompassed 2.3% of the labour force in 2016, which has only slightly increased in the last 10 years. A problem with this definition is that it does not include the self-employed, those working fewer hours than they would prefer and so on.

Changes in labour market policies that reduce coverage or entitlement in case of unemployment, and (as already indicated in Chapter 2) the risk to welfare states of the erosion of support to the middle class, can both have further consequences for welfare state legitimacy (for an example of the development in Germany, see Bothfeld and Rosenthal, 2018). In relation to pensions, the reduction in public pensions and increase in occupational pensions cause a deepening of welfare dualism so that those who are more often outsiders than insiders are less covered (Grødem et al, 2018).

The dualisation of the labour market and social divisions are not only influenced by technological development (as shown in Figure 4.1) (on the impact of technological developments on jobs, see also Frey and Osborne, 2013; McKinsey&Company, 2017; Arntz et al, 2016; Hawksworth et al, 2018; Manyika et al, 2017). The growing internationalisation of economies, which also influences what can be produced in a country, also influences local labour markets (see more in the next section).

Globalisation and Europeanisation: migrants as a threat to nationals

As argued earlier in the chapter, the lack of a job has a high risk of reducing well-being for those hit by the changes. Historically, this has been a debate not only about new technology, but also about, and related to, increased international economic interdependency. The movement of production from countries with high levels of wages to countries with lower levels as part of the impact of globalisation has also led to the loss of jobs, especially within traditional industrial production. Again, there have been winners, as in the classical economy theory of gains from trade, but people have also been sacked because of this development, and this can even be people who have worked in the sector for a long time. Richer societies and those getting a job as a result of this development could be satisfied, whereas those losing out could blame globalisation for their misfortune. This easily leads to a 'them and us' type of understanding, and thereby opens up the way for populist arguments about a return to focusing on the nation-state first. This is shown, for example, by the impact of increased trade with China on the US, which has caused fewer jobs in industries most exposed to import competition, lower lifetime incomes and higher job churning compared to other parts of society (Autor et al, 2016). Again, even if this has been beneficial for society as a whole, there have been segments of society that have lost out. The stories presented in Chapter 6 confirm this. Although the use of robots might cause a return of some production, not many jobs will be returning.

The outsourcing of production to low-wage countries is thus one way that jobs might be lost, especially for people with low levels of education. When the free movement of workers is possible, as within the EU, then those migrating and willing to work at a lower wage level than national workers can be seen as a threat by these groups of workers. The discussion in Europe on rights to social benefits, which was also part of the Brexit debate, illustrates this point (Martinsen et al, 2018). The visibility of persons from other countries might be more telling than information about the possible economic impact of free movement. There can thus also be tipping points where the size of migration has an impact on voting for populist parties (Podobnik et al, 2017).

Recent years have seen not only an impact on especially low-skilled jobs due to globalisation, but also stronger competition for jobs due to migration and, in the EU, the free movement of workers, especially from Eastern Europe. Even though the free movement of workers in the EU is positive from a macro point of view, in several countries, this has increased negative attitudes towards migrant workers. This is because many of those migrating have been argued to be working for a lower wage level than national workers, leading to what some see as social dumping, although others see it as a natural part of competition. Although social dumping is a slippery concept with a high level of ambiguity, it is also the case that 'in the short term social dumping is likely to exert downward pressure on wages and working conditions' (Bernaciak, 2014: 25), and even some who would have accepted the present level of wages risk losing competitiveness if they do not follow the downward trend.

However, whether it is social dumping or international economic competition that reduces the real wage level for some in the labour market (or even makes them redundant), it opens the way for a discussion on 'them' (those in or from other countries getting the jobs) and 'us' (losing our jobs). So, although there might be positive overall societal gains through migration (for a Danish example, see Martinsen and Rotger, 2016), the gains might not be evenly spread. This might then lead to a demand for policies that can reduce the right to enter a country and the place for migrants and the free movement of workers in different countries. A contradiction is that those migrating for jobs are often in a more precarious position in the labour market than natives (Pulignano et al, 2015; Netto and Craig, 2017), and thus perhaps not as well off as perceived by some of those who are against free movement.

Furthermore, some studies (although not including development in recent years) seem to indicate that 'because college educated individuals are much more mobile than other workers and they are likely to create opportunities for the receiving economy, immigration is likely to help native wages and employment' (Docquier et al, 2011: 23). Overall, there does not seem to be an indication at the aggregate level of any correlation between unemployment and immigration rates (Constant, 2014). However, this again points to the fact that even if this is the case at the macro-level, this might not be the perceived situation for those who have lost their job or experienced wage level pressures, which might be the consequence of a growing labour supply.

The increase in precarious positions for some can, thereby, cause a negative stance towards those who use their options for a better life by moving around and, together with the increase in refugees in the last few years in Europe, can thus help in explaining why some voters feel that they are paying the price for open economies. It has also been argued that economic globalisation would produce an economic backlash as 'low-skilled workers are *unambiguously* worse off as a result of trade liberalization' (Rodrik, 2017: 5, emphasis in original), even though, in principle, those worse off could be compensated by those gaining from globalisation. Nevertheless, if they do not compensate, then support for populism could increase. At the same time, the position of trade unions as a countervailing institutional force has been weakened (Bernaciak et al, 2014).

A possible consequence of globalisation and more open economies could be that some would be more in favour of individualisation

(Koster, 2014), and therefore would want a lesser degree of spending on social protection. Workfare (often labelled by some active labour market policy) has been on the rise in several countries (Deeming, 2014; Jordan, 2018), at least until the financial crisis (Bonoli, 2013). Although there has not been any clear sign of a social investment strategy in active labour market policy after the financial crisis, there has been an emphasis on workfarism as part of the development (Bengtsson et al, 2017). This might partly be ascribed to the fact that the effectiveness of active labour market policy, if in place at all as it is not in many countries, can increasingly be questioned (Martin, 2014; Caliendo and Schmidl, 2016; Vooren et al, 2016; Nordlund and Greve, 2018). Thus, those on the margins of the labour market might not have the feeling that they are supported to gain a foothold in the labour market, and even that part of the activation is used more as a stick as 'the effects for public work programs are clearly negative' and 'harsh monitoring and sanctioning schemes result in negative employment outcomes' (Caliendo and Schmidl, 2016: 1, 16). In this way, active labour market policy has moved from a more enabling approach to a stronger focus on work first and a disciplinary approach (Dean, 2007; Edmiston et al, 2017). One could sum it up by arguing that the winners from globalisation, or those seen as having a supranational identification, have a more positive view on immigration than those who are losers, or at least feel that they are and who perceive regional and global development as a threat (Teney et al, 2014). This naturally leads to variations in how one wants the state to intervene and to what degree, and how one looks at migrants in different societies; thereby, this can also be witnessed as a dividing line in society. Therefore, global mobility, despite having a positive macroeconomic impact, might weaken support for the welfare state.

Conclusion

Increasingly, we have seen labour market developments towards, however it is labelled, a stronger split between stable, high-quality and often well-paid jobs, and unstable, low-quality and low-paid jobs. The difference between people with various levels of educational attainment, in specific regional areas or in sectors of society in decline is a reminder of the tendency towards a more split labour market in many countries. This further leads to less socially cohesive societies, where some might see central institutions as not providing them with support, or perhaps even supporting others to get a job, maybe even what they consider to be their job. The consequences of this might be increased if the welfare state does not compensate and/or help in ensuring a decent standard of living through unemployment benefits and/or social assistance at a reasonable level. Thus, the change in the labour market could cause strong pressures on the welfare state, making it even more open for viewpoints that benefits should be targeted at the native population who have been working in the country and are thereby more deserving of benefits.

For some, the free movement of workers and globalisation (regionalisation) influence their job opportunities, and they see this more as a threat than an opportunity, a position supported by those already having the best options in society. The implication here is that they will be less supportive of the welfare state and, as a consequence, will also be prepared to support people who, at least on the rhetorical level, support nation-states, rather than those supporting a more European or global development. However, overall, it seems that the more generous welfare states also grant immigrants easier access to benefits (Römer, 2017), although the data that this builds on are from the time period 1980–2010, and support seems to have been reduced since. This is a further indication that ensuring jobs and options, including low levels of unemployment, can be an important aspect for welfare state development, and might reduce support for more populist viewpoints.

Notes

[1] This book contains many references to the debate on technology and labour market development, which will therefore not be repeated here.

[2] See: http://ec.europa.eu/eurostat/web/products-eurostat-news/-/DDN-20180209-1?inheritRedirect=true&redirect=%2Feurostat%2F (accessed 11 February 2012).

References

Arntz, M., Gregory, T. and Zierahn, U. (2016) The risk of automation for jobs in OECD countries: a comparative analysis. OECD Social, Employment and Migration Working Papers No. 189, Paris. Available at: https://doi.org/10.1787/5jlz9h56dvq7-en

Autor, D., Dorn, D. and Hanson, G. (2016) The China shock: learning from labor-market adjustment to large changes in trade. *Annual Review of Economics*, 8: 205–40.

Avent, R. (2017) *The wealth of humans: Work and its absence in the twenty-first century*. London: Penguin.

Bengtsson, M., De la Porte, C. and Jacobsson, K. (2017) Labour market policy under conditions of permanent austerity: any sign of social investment?, *Social Policy & Administration*, 51(2): 367–88.

Bernaciak, M. (2014) Social dumping and the EU integration process. Working Paper 2014.06 ETUI.

Bernaciak, M., Gumbrell-McCormick, R. and Hyman, R. (2014) European trade unionism: from crisis to renewal? Report 133, ETUI.

Bonoli, G. (2013) *The origins of active social policy: Labour market and childcare policies in comparative perspective*. Oxford: Oxford University Press.

Bothfeld, S. and Rosenthal, P. (2018) The end of social security as we know it – the erosion of status protection in German labour market policy. *Journal of Social Policy*, 47(2), 275–94.

Caliendo, M. and Schmidl, R. (2016) Youth unemployment and active labor market policies in Europe. *IZA Journal of Labor Policy*, 5(1): 1–30.

Chung, H. (2016) Dualization and subjective employment insecurity: explaining the subjective employment insecurity divide between permanent and temporary workers across 23 European countries. *Economic and Industrial Democracy*, pp 1–30, DOI: 10.1177/0143831X16656411.

Chung, H. (2018) Dualization and the access to occupational family-friendly working-time arrangements across Europe. *Social Policy & Administration*, 52(2): 491–507.

Clark, A. and Oswald, A. (1994) Unhappiness and unemployment. *The Economic Journal*, 104(424): 648–59.

Classen, T. and Dunn, R. (2012) The effect of job loss and unemployment duration on suicide risk in the United States: a new look using mass-layoffs and unemployment duration. *Health Economics*, 21: 338–50.

Constant, A. (2014) Do migrants take the jobs of native workers? IZA World of Labor, issue 10.

Cortes, G.M. (2016) Where have the middle-wage workers gone? A study of polarization using panel data. *Journal of Labor Economics*, 34(1): 63–105.

Dean, H. (2007) The ethics of welfare-to-work. *Policy & Politics*, 35(4): 573–89.

Deeming, C. (2014) Foundations of the workfare state – reflections on the political transformation of the welfare state in Britain. *Social Policy & Administration*, 49(7): 862–86.

Docquier, F., Ozden, C. and Peri, G. (2011) *The labor market effects of immigration and emigration in OECD countries*. Discussion Paper No. 6258, Bonn: IZA.

Easterlin, R. (2013) Happiness, growth and public policy. IZA Discussion Paper, No. 7234, IZA.

Edmiston, D., Patrick, R. and Garthwaite, K. (2017) Introduction: Austerity, welfare and social citizenship. *Social Policy & Society*, 16(2): 253–9.

Emmenegger, P., Häusermann, S., Palier, B. and Seeleib-Kaiser, M. (2012) *The age of dualization: The changing face of inequality in deindustrializing societies.* Oxford: Oxford University Press.

Foged, M. and Peri, G. (2015) Immigrants' effect on native workers: new analysis on longitudinal data. IZA, Discussion Paper DP No. 8961.

Frey, B.S. and Stutzer, A. (2010) Happiness a new approach in economics. CESifo Dice report. *Journal for Institutional Comparisons*, 8(4): 3–36.

Frey, C. and Osborne, M. (2013) The future of employment: how susceptible are jobs to computerisation? Oxford, Oxford Department of Engineering Science, Oxford University.

Frey, C. and Stutzer, A. (2002) Happiness and economics: How the economy and institutions affect well-being. Princeton, NJ: Princeton University Press.

Goos, M., Manning, A. and Salomons, A. (2014) Explaining job polarization: routine-based technological change and offshoring. *American Economic Review*, 104(8): 2509–26.

Greve, B. (2017) *Technology and the future of work: The impact on labour markets and welfare states.* Cheltenham: Edward Elgar.

Grødem, A., Hagelund, J. and Hippe, J. (2018) Beyond coverage: the politics of occupational pension and the role of trade unions. Introduction to special issue. *Transfer*, 24(1): 9–23.

Hawksworth, J., Berriman, R. and Goel, S. (2018) Will robots really steal our jobs? An international analysis of the potential long term impact of automation, PricewaterhouseCooper. Available at: www.pwc.co.uk/economic-services/assets/international-impact-of-automation-feb-2018.pdf

Hill, S. (2015) *Raw deal: How the 'Uber economy' and runaway capitalism are screwing American workers.* New York, NY: St. Martin's Press.

Jordan, J. (2018) Welfare grunters and workfare monsters? An empirical review of the operation of two UK 'Work Programme' centres. *Journal of Social Policy*, 47(3): 583–601.

Keune, M. (2018) Opportunity or threat? How trade union power and preferences shape occupational pensions. *Social Policy & Administration*, 52(2): 473–86.

Koster, F. (2014) Economic openness and welfare state attitudes: a multilevel study across 67 countries. *International Journal of Welfare*, 23: 128–38.

Layard, R. (2005) *Happiness. Lessons from a new science*. London: Penguin.

Manyika, J., Lund, S., Chui, M., Bughin, J., Woetzel, J., Batra, P., Ko, R. and Sanghvi, S. (2017) Jobs lost, jobs gained: workforce transitions in a time of automation. Available at: www.mckinsey. com/~/media/mckinsey/featured%20insights/Future%20of%20 Organizations/What%20the%20future%20of%20work%20will%20 mean%20for%20jobs%20skills%20and%20wages/MGI-Jobs-Lost-Jobs-Gained-Report-December-6-2017.ashx (accessed 7 May 2018).

Martin, J. (2014) Activation and active labour market policies in OECD countries: stylized facts and evidence on their effectiveness. IZA Policy Paper No. 84.

Martinsen, D. and Rotger, G. (2016) The fiscal impact of EU immigration on the universalistic welfare state. Working Paper No. 6, 2016, København, SFI.

Martinsen, D., Rotger, G. and Sampson Thierry, J. (2018) Free movement of people and cross-border welfare in the European Union: dynamic rules, limited outcomes. *Journal of European Social Policy*, first published 30 May. Available at: https://doi. org/10.1177/0958928718767300

McKinsey&Company (2017) Shaping the future of work in Europe's digital front-runners. Available at: www.mckinsey.com/~/media/ mckinsey/featured%20insights/europe/shaping%20the%20future%20 of%20work%20in%20europes%20nine%20digital%20front%20 runner%20countries/shaping-the-future-of-work-in-europes-digital-front-runners.ashx (accessed 8 May 2017).

Mokyr, J., Vickers, C. and Ziebarth, N.L. (2015) The history of technological anxiety and the future of economic growth: is this time different? *Journal of Economic Perspectives*, 29(3): 31–50.

Netto, G. and Craig, G. (2017) Introduction: migration and differential labour market participation. *Social Policy & Society*, 16(4): 607–11.

Nordlund, M. and Greve, B. (2018) Active labour market policies. In B. Greve (ed) *The Routledge handbook of the welfare state* (2nd edn). Oxon: Routledge.

Palier, B. and Thelen, K. (2010) Institutionalizing dualism: complementarities and change in France and Germany. *Politics & Society*, 38(1): 119–48.

Podobnik, B., Jusup, M., Kovac, D. and Stanley, H.E. (2017) Predicting the rise of EU right-wing populism in response to unbalanced immigration. *Complexity*, pp 1–9, DOI. 10.1155/2017/1580526.

Pulignano, V., Meardi, G. and Doerflinger, N. (2015) Trade unions and labour market dualization: a comparison of policies and attitudes towards agency and migrant workers in Germany and Belgium. *Work, Employment and Society*, 29(5): 808–25.

Rodrik, D. (2017) Populism and the economics of globalization. Available at: https://drodrik.scholar.harvard.edu/files/dani-rodrik/files/populism_and_the_economics_of_globalization.pdf (accessed 9 January 2018).

Römer, F. (2017) Generous to all or 'insiders only'? The relationship between welfare state generosity and immigrants' welfare rights. *Journal of European Social Policy*, 27(2): 173–96.

Schwartz, B. (2004) *The paradox of choice. Why more is less*. New York, NY: Harper Collins.

Seeleib-Kaiser, M. (2013) Welfare systems in Europe and the United States. Conservative Germany converging toward the liberal US model? *International Journal of Social Quality*, 3(2): 60–77.

Seeleib-Kaiser, M. (2016) The end of the conservative German welfare state model. *Social Policy & Administration*, 50(2): 219–40.

Standing, G. (2011) *The new dangerous class*. London: Bloomsbury.

Standing, G. (2014) *A precariat charter: From denizens to citizens*. London: Bloomsbury.

Teney, C., Lacewell, O. and Wilde, P. (2014) Winners and losers of globalization in Europe: attitudes and ideologies. *European Political Science Review*, 6(4): 575–95.

Vooeren, M., Haelermans, C., Groot, W., Maassen van den Brink, H. (2016) The effectiveness of active labour market policies: a systematic meta-analysis. Available at: www.sole-jole.org/17403.pdf (accessed 9 January 2017).

Watts B. and Fitzpatrick, S. (2018) *Welfare conditionality*. Oxon: Routledge

5

What form has the development in welfare spending taken?

Introduction

The possible development in welfare state spending is often described using labels such as 'retrenchment', 'austerity', 'the use of new public management' and 'marketisation'. Research is often further conducted on a single country or issue, and less by trying to encapsulate the varieties of development in a number of countries, both on an overall level and within certain specific elements of welfare state development. However, given the focus on aspects such as welfare chauvinism and populism (as shown in Chapter Two), and also deserving/undeservingness, it is very important to be able to distinguish between actual and possible types of retrenchment, or changes that are due to, for example, demographic developments, the cost of providing services and the replacement rates of central benefits, as this can also add knowledge on whether changes are driven by the ideas of neoliberalism and/or welfare chauvinism. Furthermore, at the outset, right-wing populism could be expected to reduce spending and cut taxes.

This implies the need to look into the size of the overall spending on welfare as a percentage of the total economy, measured by gross domestic product (GDP), as this is one indicator of whether social policy is actually declining or not in relative terms, albeit that it cannot stand alone. This chapter tries to depict the development from before the financial crisis to the current time, insofar as comparative data are available.

The second section presents the overall depiction of the development in welfare state spending using a variety of parameters, and the third section looks into the development in replacement rates, discussing possible ways of carrying out retrenchment by changing conditionality (eligibility criteria, the size of benefits and the use of tax expenditures) (Watts and Fitzpatrick, 2018). The fourth section then considers the development in areas where, at the outset, one should not expect retrenchment – health care and old age – as they are connected to, and have higher support from, voters (although see also Chapter Seven), and are thereby also often supported by more populist parties as the benefit is not perceived as going to those not contributing. The fifth section then makes some conclusions.

Central data on the development

This section presents central data on the development in European welfare states representing varieties of welfare regimes (see Kennet and Lendvai-Baiton, 2017; Greve, 2019) as this depicts and indicates how the development has been carried out and whether this can be theoretically argued to have influenced the legitimacy of welfare states. Naturally, it is not always easy to find solid data, and approaches can be different, so that different databases might cause different results. for a comparison of the Social Citizenship Program (SCIP) and the Comparative Welfare Entitlementsdataset (CWED), see, for example, Bolukbasi and Öktem (2018), who also argue that 'the analysis of welfare state retrenchment appears to depend much, alas, on dataset choice' (Bolukbasi and Öktem, 2018: 97). Figure 5.1 shows a snapshot of the difference in spending on social protection among EU countries.

Figure 5.1 depicts strong variation in spending as a percentage of GDP among countries within the European Union (EU), from more than one third to less than one sixth of GDP. This reflects different political priorities in the countries, but also variations in economic options to develop and/or continue existing policies in the different welfare states. The figure contrasts with the classical depiction of who the high spenders are, with France at the top, but with high levels of spending also in countries such as Belgium and Italy. This reflects the fact that the figure is based on gross spending data. One issue is what the situation actually was in 2015, but another is the development in spending over and through the financial crisis.

Table 5.1 presents the proportion of GDP spent on social policy for the selected countries since 2005. Countries represent classical welfare regimes (Nordic, Continental, liberal), as well as Eastern and Southern European countries (Greve, 2019). The data include the last year before the financial crisis up to the most recent data available.

Table 5.1 shows variation in Europe, with Eastern Europe and liberal welfare states spending less on welfare than the other regime types, albeit that there has been some catching up, especially in Southern Europe. France seems to be the highest spender and even Italy spends more than Sweden; however, it is important to be aware that the impact of the tax system can influence the picture (Adema and

Figure 5.1: Social protection expenditures as a proportion of GDP, 2015 or latest years

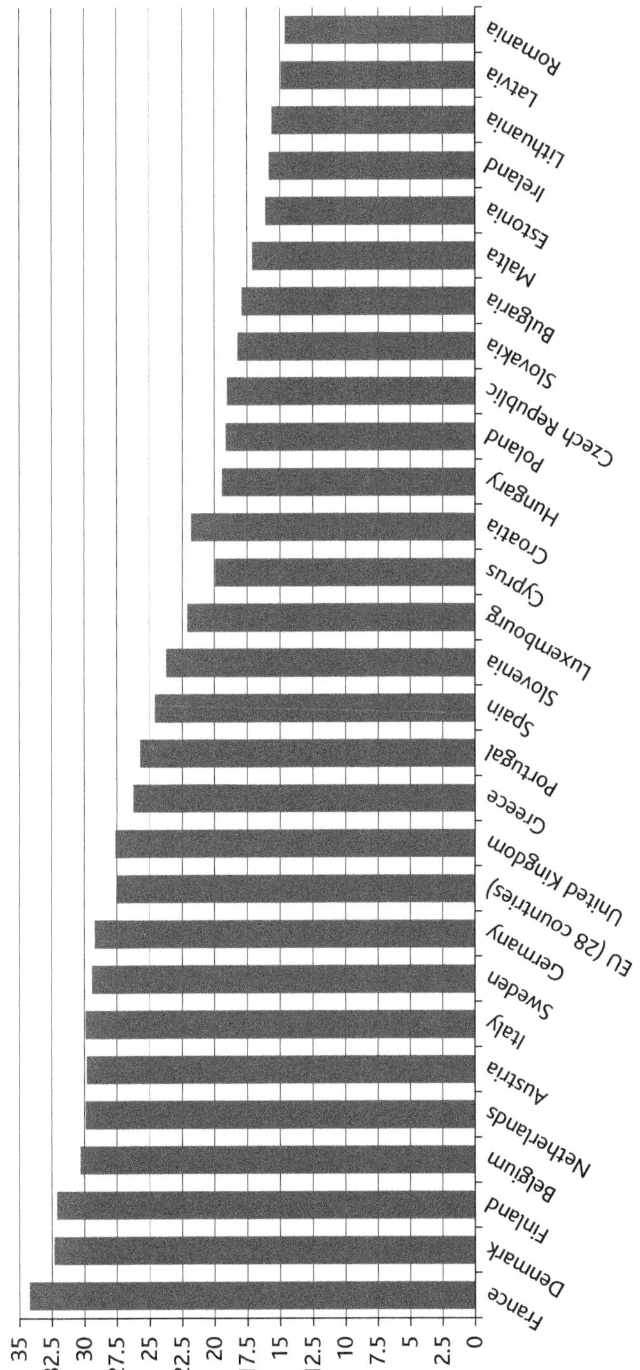

Source: http://ec.europa.eu/eurostat/tgm/graph.do?tab=graph&plugin=1&pcode=tps00098&language=en&toolbox=sort (accessed 15 August 2018)

Table 5.1: Spending on social protection as percentages of GDP in selected EU countries, 2006–15

	2006	2008	2010	2012	2014	2015
Nordic:						
Denmark	28.4	28.9	32.4	32.0	32.8	32.3
Sweden	28.6	27.7	28.6	29.3	29.5	29.2
Continental:						
Germany	27.8	27.1	29.8	28.7	29.0	29.1
France	30.4	30.4	32.9	33.5	34.2	33.9
Liberal:						
Ireland	17.5	20.7	25.2	24.4	21.6	16.3
UK	25.1	25.8	29.0	29.1	27.3	28.6
Southern Europe:						
Spain	20.0	21.4	24.6	25.5	25.4	24.6
Italy	25.6	26.7	28.9	29.3	29.9	29.9
Eastern Europe:						
Czech Republic	17.6	17.9	20.0	20.4	19.7	19.0
Poland	19.7	19.3	19.7	18.9	19.1	–

Source: EUROSTAT, spr_exp_sum (accessed 13 August 2018)

Ladaique, 2009), so that when taking taxation, voluntary contributions and tax expenditures into consideration, the picture can be and is very different.[1] However, this is less of a problem when trying to show the development over time as, for example, for all years, there has been a difference in the taxation of benefit. Thus, even if only part of the picture, Table 5.1 is an indication of whether there have been sufficient resources available for the purpose of fulfilling the need and demand for services within social policy. The data are also and will be influenced by the development in GDP. For example, the risk is that a possible increase in the overall level of spending from 2008 to 2010, in the wake of the financial crisis, reflects a reduction in GDP more than an increase in spending. This thereby helps in explaining that in all countries, social protection increased as a proportion of GDP from 2008 to 2010; however, since then, most countries have had only very limited change,[2] although in many countries, there has been a real increase in spending (see later). In a longer time perspective, this is also the case from the year 2000 (Greve, 2014).

The increase in spending is, partly, in some countries, also a consequence of the fact that the need for social spending increases in times of crisis as a kind of automatic stabiliser in economies. This increase in spending, if not accompanied by an increase in taxation, combined with the economic support to banks to avoid them going bankrupt, explains the growing public sector deficit in most countries. This, as discussed later in the book, was then used in some countries to argue for a reduction in overall spending in order to reduce the budget deficit and, if possible, also the level of state debt.

Part of the reason for the expansion in expenditure could have been a change in unemployment as this rose after the financial crisis. Thus, Table 5.2 shows spending on unemployment (both active and passive labour market policy) as a percentage of GDP.

As can be witnessed from the table, in most countries, the increase in spending on unemployment was part of the reason for the increase in spending on social policy from 2008 to 2010. However, it does not explain the then more stable development as there has, in fact, been a reduction in spending on unemployment since 2010 in most of the countries, causing an increase in spending in other welfare areas. The picture confirms a stronger northern focus on labour market policies, albeit that there has also been a catching up from Southern Europe in this area, and also a high increase in Ireland, although in 2015, only reaching the level of 2008. However, there might also be data problems in the field related to issues such as accounting, different levels of government delivering it and also the quality of the service (Clasen et al, 2016), as well as change in GDP. However, over time, it still reflects a pattern of development.

Table 5.2: Spending on unemployment as a percentage of GDP for selected EU countries, 2006–15

GEO/TIME	2006	2008	2010	2012	2014	2015
Nordic:						
Denmark	2.0	1.0	1.9	1.9	1.6	1.5
Sweden	1.5	0.8	1.3	1.2	1.1	1.1
Continental:						
Germany	1.8	1.4	1.6	1.1	1.1	1.0
France	1.7	1.5	1.9	2.0	2.0	2.0
Liberal:						
Ireland	1.3	1.8	3.7	3.3	2.6	1.9
UK	0.6	0.6	0.7	0.7	0.5	0.4
Southern Europe:						
Spain	2.1	2.3	3.2	3.4	2.7	2.2
Italy	0.5	1.1	1.5	1.6	1.7	1.7
Eastern Europe:						
Czech Republic	0.5	0.6	0.8	0.6	0.6	0.5
Poland	0.6	0.4	0.4	0.3	0.2	–

Source: EUROSTAT, spr_exp_sum (accessed 13 August 2018)

The continuation of the same level of spending since 2010 must, therefore, have other reasons, and cannot be attributed only to the change in unemployment. However (and this is returned to later), the low and only brief increase in the level of spending on unemployment might also be due to the fact that there has been a reduction in income transfers (see later) to the unemployed, which can help in explaining the development.

Proportions of GDP, either overall or for individual subsections, do not inform us as to the real level of development. Therefore, one needs to look into the real development in spending, for example, by discounting using the inflation rate, which is presented in Table 5.3.

In Table 5.3, the difference in the overall level of spending between countries reflects both the proportion of GDP devoted to social policy, and also the size of the economies in different countries. Looked upon in this way, the data indicate that, with the exception of Ireland, Italy and Spain, after 2010, there has been a growth in resources available for welfare states. Overall, this result was also achieved for an analysis of the time period from 2000 to 2013 for a number of EU countries (more or less the same as earlier, but also including the US), indicating that, with the exception of Greece, there has been a real growth in

Table 5.3: Spending on social protection in million euros in constant 2010 prices for selected EU countries, 2006–15

GEO/TIME	2006	2008	2010	2012	2014	2015
Nordic:						
Denmark	69.894	72.656	78.887	78.632	83.559	83.640
Sweden	101.350	101.670	105.393	109.604	114.470	118.886
Continental:						
Germany	699.460	708.406	768.797	765.456	799.109	827.333
France	591.379	609.152	658.094	680.700	708.950	717.462
Liberal:						
Ireland	30.992	35.668	42.217	41.773	40.279	40.681
UK	469.490	487.477	533.267	544.360	537.927	575.816
Southern Europe:						
Spain	218.483	241.771	266.224	252.567	248.222	251.039
Italy	421.412	440.601	462.938	452.603	459.292	467.410
Eastern Europe:						
Czech Republic	26.870	28.990	31.403	31.431	31.679	32.390
Poland	59.666	65.785	71.307	71.048	75.805	–

Source: EUROSTAT, spr_exp_sum (accessed 13 August 2018)

spending and even tendencies towards convergence across the various types of welfare states (Greve, 2014).

In addition, this measure, despite clearly at the macro-level, informing on whether there has been an increase in available resources in real terms, is not related to the potential number of users of benefits within a specific area. Therefore, in principle, one would need more detailed knowledge of the development of the real resources available to deliver services for each person within different segments of the welfare state. This is the case in Table 5.4, which describes the resources available per inhabitant for all welfare areas, and therefore only partly reflecting the available resources within each specific policy field. In order to also ensure that the picture can be confirmed for a longer time span, spending in constant prices per inhabitant is also included for the year 2000.

Table 5.4 shows a development where, overall, in all countries, there have been more resources available per inhabitant in fixed prices over the period from 2000. Since 2010, in a few countries (Spain, Italy and Ireland), there has been a slight decline, as also indicated in Table 5.3. Given the change in demography and the variation between fixed and flexible costs for the delivery of services, this might not necessarily be looked upon by the individual as an improvement. This

Table 5.4: Spending on social protection in euros per inhabitant in 2010 prices in selected EU countries, 2000–15

GEO/TIME	2000	2006	2008	2010	2012	2014	2015
Nordic:							
Denmark	9.384	12.855	13.226	14.220	14.063	14.728	14.606
Sweden	9.006	11.161	11.028	11.238	11.514	11.822	12.115
Continental:							
Germany	7.396	8.490	8.627	9.400	9.513	9.877	10.129
France	7.038	9.322	9.491	10.153	10.402	10.721	10.769
Liberal:							
Ireland	3.683	7.357	8.000	9.258	9.110	8.696	8.716
UK	7.184	7.745	7.909	8.491	8.571	8.344	8.930
Southern Europe:							
Spain	3.107	4.910	5.252	5.716	5.467	5.403	5.469
Italy	5.177	7.248	7.490	7.810	7.601	7.561	7.698
Eastern Europe:							
Czech Republic	1.170	2.630	2.794	2.998	3.000	3.019	3.076
Poland	954	1.564	1.725	1.874	1.867	1.976	–

Source: EUROSTAT, spr_exp_sum (accessed 13 August 2018)

is because, for example, fewer children in day care might increase the average cost per child because fixed cost (buildings, heating, etc) will still have to be paid. In other areas, an increase in the number of people needing support, for example, in health care, might increase costs. It is mainly in the field of income transfers that changes in the number of recipients has a direct impact on overall spending, being less so within the other fields. Still, it raises the issue of whether there has been retrenchment, as often argued in the welfare state literature (for a recent example, see Taylor-Gooby et al, 2017), or whether, in reality, retrenchment is the subjective perception of the development due to adaptation, as well as given that change in demography and ambitions to cover new areas have also caused reductions, for example, in replacement rates (see later). Still, if the subjective perception of the development is of reductions, this might reduce the legitimacy of the welfare state. However, in general, there does not seem to be support for the view that populist right-wing parties support retrenchment overall, nor deregulation (Roth et al, 2018).

Even spending per inhabitant in fixed prices might not be a very precise description of what has happened in all cases. Thus, for example, taking long-term care (LTC) for the elderly as an example, the case could be that those expected to be in need for care have had improvements in their health as a consequence of the tendencies both to live longer and also to have increased disability-free adjusted life-years (Greve, 2017). Other tendencies within a policy area might also have an impact on the need for resources. Again, using LTC and social investment (Morel et al, 2012; Midgley et al, 2017), this could imply that spending that has reduced the need for care through rehabilitation and the use of welfare technology (Greve, 2018a) has also reduced the need for LTC (see further later). Therefore, a reduction in spending does not necessarily cause a reduction in the quality of service and/or quality of life given that the elderly, in general, prefer to stay as long as possible in their own homes (Wiles et al, 2012; Aspinal et al, 2016), and thus investment making this possible will reduce the need for care. Naturally, within the field of LTC, it might not be a total reduction in the need for care, but it could possibly reduce overall need (Greve, 2018a). Thus, the interpretation of the data is not an easy task. Still, in many ways, using the preceding data, combined with the development of the replacement rate, is a good indicator of how and whether we have witnessed retrenchment in welfare states.

There seems to be a movement where the focus has been more on classical social protection, although the crisis (data are up to 2014) seems to have caused a slowdown in social investment expenditures, which can be explained by the fact that continued expansion here might have jeopardised spending on more classical social protection. The data do not give any indication of overall retrenchment, with variation, even when taking the target population of the different spending functions into consideration (Ronchi, 2018).

Change from the direct delivery of social services to giving families an economic benefit to buy services can also blur the development as this, in principle, might reduce spending on services but also increase spending on income transfers. However, this can be disentangled by looking into how the development of the replacement rate has been carried out for different central benefits, such as unemployment, social assistance and old-age pensions (this is returned to later).

The individual's perception of the development in well-being and quality of life depends not only on welfare state spending, but also on the development in incomes enabling the purchase of goods and services in the private household. The impact of this ability to buy products is stronger in less universal welfare states, but might still be there as well. Therefore, the development towards the dualisation of the labour market (Emmenegger et al, 2012) further implies that those not close to the labour market will have had a slower development than depicted in Table 5.5, which has a focus on how real wages, for example, the buying power of nominal wages corrected by the inflation rate, have developed since 2006.

The picture in Table 5.5 is very diverse, with a few countries in Eastern Europe (Poland and the Czech Republic) having a relatively high increase overall, but with a more mixed picture in other countries, and seemingly not really linked to the welfare model. However, there is a tendency towards lower real wage development in the liberal welfare states and in countries with an already higher average level of wages, presumably indirectly causing a convergence within Europe. This needs to be contrasted with, for example, average real wages in the US in 2014, which were 7% higher than in 1979, although those in the 95th percentile had had an increase of 45% (Avent, 2017).

One could look, instead, at real minimum wages as this will reflect to a larger degree income development for the working class and those with a more precarious position in the labour market. This is done in Table 5.6.

The table shows that there has been a slight increase in the minimum income since 2006 in most countries, and a high increase in Poland, in particular, but less so in the higher-income countries and with tendencies towards stagnation in the liberal countries of Ireland and the US. The table also shows that in the wake of the financial crisis, there

Table 5.5: Mean real wage monthly development in each year since 2006 in selected EU countries and the US

Country	2006	2007	2008	2009	2010	2011	2012	2013	2014	2015
Nordic:										
Denmark	1.1	2.1	1	1.7	0.9	−0.5	−0.4	0.3	0.6	1.1
Sweden	1.4	0.9	1.8	3	0.4	−0.4	2.1	2.5	2.8	2
Continental:										
France	−0.6	1.2	−1.1	0.3	−1.3	1.8	1	2.1	0.8	1.1
Germany	−1	−0.8	−0.4	−0.2	1.3	1	0.6	0.5	1.9	2.8
Liberal:										
Ireland	3.7	−1.3	1	1.8	−0.3	−1.8	−1.4	−1.2	−0.5	1.9
UK		0.7	0.8	−0.5	−1.9	−3.6	−1.9	−0.5	−1.4	1.3
Southern Europe:										
Italy	0.8	0.1	−0.6	−0.6	0.6	−1.9	−4.2	−0.4	0.2	1
Spain	1.2	1.2	1	3.5	−0.9	−2.1	−3	−1.4	0.1	1.6
Eastern Europe:										
Poland	3.8	5.3	5.6	1.9	1.3	1.3	0	2.7	3.3	4.2
Czech Republic	3.1	4.4	0.7	0.2	−0.7		−1.7	−0.7	1.9	3.4
USA	1.1	1	−1.1	1.4	0.7	−0.3	0.3	0.4	0.7	2.2

Source: ILO (accessed 14 August 2018)

Table 5.6: Development in the minimum income in US dollars, in fixed 2017 prices, in selected EU member states and the US, selected years, 2006–17

Country	2006	2008	2010	2012	2014	2016	2017
Czech Republic	8,023.8	7,559.2	7,374.4	7,005.3	7,312.5	8,433.0	9,145.8
France	19,433.6	19,668.4	19,879.6	20,110.6	20,306.4	20,559.3	20,538.7
Germany	–	–	–	–	–	21,070.4	21,544.6
Ireland	17,333.3	17,955.1	18,971.7	18,190.1	18,065.1	19,163.3	19,307.0
Poland	7,071.9	8,299.3	9,116.9	9,618.9	10,661.7	11,923.3	12,627.9
Spain	14,172.3	14,695.1	15,280.6	14,638.2	12,468.1	14,873.0	15,755.8
UK	16,702.5	17,149.9	17,173.4	16,877.9	16,933.7	17,762.2	17,988.6
USA	13,024.9	14,579.5	16,951.7	16,099.7	15,614.0	15,401.2	15,080.0

Note: Data for Denmark, Italy and Sweden were not available.

Source: OECD statistics. Available at: https://stats.oecd.org/Index.aspx?DataSetCode=RMW# (accessed 14 August 2018)

has been stagnation in most countries, and even a decline in Spain (albeit catching up in 2017) and the US. Thus, those most pressured by the financial crisis in relation to unemployment and job insecurity have also witnessed pressure on the real wage level, and thereby their standard of living. For the period from 2001 to 2012, there was not:

> a general decrease in minimum wages. Still, minimum wages in countries where these were low at the start of the observation period caught up to some extent, whereas the minimum wages in the more generous countries lost ground relative to average living standards. (Marchal and Marx, 2018: 30)

This shows that those in more unstable jobs (see Chapter 4) have lost ground, which helps in explaining attitudes and support for populist parties (as seen in Chapter 6).

This points to the fact that, given the overall economic development, an increase in inequality can be witnessed (see Chapter 3), which might feed back into the position of and possible support for more populist political parties. A core issue for welfare states and how they cope with decommodification is the level of the replacement rate, which is the focus of the next section.

Changes in replacement rates – and why

Development in replacement rates is central to understand how the situation has changed for those dependent on welfare benefits, and whether the overall absolute increase in spending reflects better living conditions for some of those on the margin of the welfare state. Here, the choice is to look at unemployment and pensions due to the possible difference in support for them. The focus is on the period since 2006 in order to include the possible impact of the financial crisis. Historically, there have been growing replacement rates since 1950, with a peak in the mid-1970s or late 1980s in several countries (Ervik et al, 2015). Table 5.7 shows the development of replacement rates in the first period of unemployment for a single earner with median income since 2006.

With the exception of the reductions in Spain, Sweden and the US, the table does not indicate any strong changes in the replacement rate for those becoming unemployed, and even an increase in the Czech Republic and Italy. However, the table does not paint the full picture as changes in the requirements for getting benefit and the length of benefit can also influence the situation. Furthermore, if there is real wage increases, especially for those with high incomes, a constant replacement rate will cause a relative reduction in the

Table 5.7: Net replacement rate for a single earner, 100% median income from 2006 to 2016, initial period, selected EU countries and the US

Country	2006	2008	2010	2012	2014	2015	2016
Czech Republic	50	50	65	65	65	65	65
Denmark	59.7	57.9	58.1	58.3	58.7	58.6	58
France	66.6	66.5	66.4	66.4	66.5	67.8	67.9
Germany	61.8	60.3	59.6	59	58.8	58.9	59
Ireland	33.8	36.4	38.1	35.1	35.2	34.4	33.4
Italy	58.2	57.2	56.5	56.3	60.5	65.6	64.3
Poland	33.7	28.8	35	34	32.1	31	30
Spain	61.2	61.1	59.6	57.6	55.9	55.7	55.1
Sweden	61.3	50.3	46.9	44.7	42.2	41.6	53
UK	13	12.7	13.3	14.1	14	13.8	13.6
USA	55.9	52.5	48.6	46.1	45.3	44.2	43.5

Source: Data from OECD.Stat (accessed 15 August 2018)

perceived standard of living of those on benefits. There are differences among countries, and not always due to historical depictions of welfare regimes. It has further been argued that, while varying starkly among countries, retrenchment took place before the financial crisis, although not hitting low-income earners, and continued after the crisis, when it affected low-income earners more (Jahn, 2017).

Furthermore, there could also be a difference between the first short period of unemployment and being long-term unemployed. Therefore, Table 5.8 shows the development for the long-term

Table 5.8: Replacement rate for a single earner, 100% median income, five years unemployed, selected EU countries and the US

Country	2006	2008	2010	2012	2014	2015	2016
Czech Republic	4.8	4.8	4.6	4.6	4.6	4.6	4.6
Denmark	47.8	46.3	23.2	23.3	32.9	32.8	32.5
France	39.2	39.4	40.2	40.1	40.2	40.8	40.7
Germany	29.6	28.6	27.8	25.3	25.3	25.3	25.2
Ireland	33.8	36.6	38.3	35.6	35.7	34.9	33.9
Italy	6.7	7.6	7.5	7.5	7.9	19.7	19.3
Poland	6.7	5.8	5.9	5.8	5.4	5.3	5.1
Spain	24.5	24.4	23.8	23.1	22.4	22.3	22
Sweden	27.1	29.4	27.4	26.1	24.6	24.3	26.9
UK	13	12.7	13.3	14.1	14	13.8	13.6
USA	5.6	11.9	18.5	15.4	3.5	3.4	3.4

Source: OECD, benefits and wages (accessed 15 August 2018)

unemployed (for at least five years), again for a single person with an income at 100% of median income.

The data again show a varied picture, with strong retrenchment in Denmark and in the US after an increase. The development in Italy from 2014 to 2016 seems to be in sharp contrast to the historical level and development of spending in Italy. This can be explained by a change in the systems in 2015, with a new unemployment assistance programme (Jessoula, 2015). Even though there are differences and no real development in some countries, there seems to be a tendency towards a lower level, which indicates retrenchment in a central welfare state benefit.

Still, to a limited extent, the data lend support to the fact that those persons in several countries who are seen as deserving had a reduction in the direct replacement rate (see more in Chapter 7). However, it also has to be seen in the light of the increasing emphasis on a work-first approach, implying that in several cases, people will not be able to get access to benefits (Dean, 2007; Bonoli, 2010).

Overall, besides the changes in unemployment benefits, in relation to social assistance, there has not been any 'large retrenchment, reforms or benefit cuts with respect to minimum income benefits' (Wang and Vliet, 2016: 351) within Organisation for Economic Co-operation and Development (OECD) countries, although the study refers to the period from 1990 to 2009, and thus does not include developments after the financial crisis. Looking into eligibility criteria for unemployment benefit, only to a limited extent does there seem to have been strong changes from 2011 to 2014, with the UK as a possible exception as conditions seem to have been tightened (Langenburcher, 2015).[3] Naturally, this may reflect the fact that in times of growing unemployment and with many affected by spells of unemployment, reducing the level of benefit might be politically difficult.

The unemployed, whether relying on unemployment benefits or social assistance, are one group for whom support for a high level of benefit is perhaps not so strong as some unemployed people are seen as not actively searching for a job and therefore undeserving. In contrast, pensioners have traditionally been seen as a group deserving of a relatively high level of benefits. Therefore, the next focus is on the replacement rate for people on pensions.

Despite the many pension reforms, there seems to be a very mixed picture of the impact on the development in the replacement rate[4] of pensions. Table 5.9 shows the development in the pension replacement rate (gross and net) for a single person entering the labour market at the age of 20, and with different income levels.

Table 5.9: Development of the gross and net replacement rate in pensions for a single person – difference between 2006 and 2012 – retiring at the national retirement age in selected EU member states

	Male						Female					
	Gross replacement rate			Net replacement rate			Gross replacement rate			Net replacement rate		
Gross earnings	0.50 of AW	1.00 of AW	1.50 of AW	0.50 of AW	1.00 of AW	1.50 of AW	0.50 of AW	1.00 of AW	1.50 of AW	0.50 of AW	1.00 of AW	1.50 of AW
Czech Republic	4.6	1.6	4.0	2.5	-0.3	1.5	4.6	1.6	4.0	2.5	-0.3	1.5
Denmark	-3.3	-1.8	-3.0	-19.5	-13.9	-15.3	-3.3	-1.8	-3.0	-19.5	-13.9	-15.3
France	3.1	5.5	-1.0	-0.3	5.8	0.7	3.1	5.5	-1.0	-0.3	5.8	0.7
Germany	-1.0	-1.0	-0.7	-4.0	-4.2	-4.2	-1.0	-1.0	-0.7	-4.0	-4.2	-4.2
Ireland	5.0	2.5	1.7	7.2	4.7	4.3	5.0	2.5	1.7	7.2	4.7	4.3
Italy	3.2	3.2	3.2	9.1	6.6	6.2	18.4	18.4	18.4	7.3	23.3	23.4
Poland	-11.9	-12.5	-12.5	-13.2	-15.3	-15.9	0.3	4.2	4.2	0.7	4.4	4.1
Spain	-7.3	-7.3	-7.3	-2.7	-4.6	-5.5	-7.3	-7.3	-7.3	-2.7	-4.6	-5.5
Sweden	-6.4	-6.0	-7.6	-10.4	-8.8	-8.3	-6.4	-6.0	-7.6	-10.4	-8.8	-8.3
UK	4.8	1.8	1.2	3.5	0.9	1.3	4.8	1.8	1.2	3.5	0.9	1.3

Note: AW = average wage.

Source: Calculated based upon data extracted from OECD.Stat (accessed 8 November 2017)

The picture emerging from the table across Europe is very different, with countries witnessing an increase in the pension replacement rate, but also retrenchment in Denmark, Germany, Spain and Sweden. Thereby, in some countries, retrenchment has taken place, whereas this has not been the case in other countries. If looking at pension wealth development from 2009 to 2014, there are both increases and decreases. It is also the case that 'almost everywhere mandated pension regimes grant the low waged relatively high replacement rates' (Meyer, 2017: 345). Meyer further argues that what we have seen is more a calibration than, in fact, austerity, so that even if insiders in the labour market are still well protected, outsiders seem not to lose as much as was once expected to be the case. However, it is also still the case that the future net replacement rate will be higher for low-income earners (50% of an average production worker's wage) than for the average wage earner (OECD, 2017). Therefore, despite reforms, there still seems to be a redistribution towards those with low income, and given the possible change in the labour market (see Chapter 4), those on the margins will still have some coverage in many countries, despite the fact that 'recent reforms will lower replacement rates in many countries due to measures aimed at improving pension finances' (OECD, 2017: 16).

On this understanding, despite this being an area with often relatively large voter support, the data on the replacement rate and its development within the pension system do not support the fact that it has been left untouched, where the option of a gradual reduction over time, for example, by 'decay', seems a more likely explanation (Saxonberg and Sirovátka, 2009). The use of invisible policy instruments such as a change in indexation rules has been the case in at least four European countries (Britain, Denmark, Finland and Germany) from 1974 to 2014, and also that '"visible" policy instruments, above all else nominal benefits, were much more likely to be used for expansionary purposes than for retrenchment' (Jensen et al, 2018: 73). However, at the same time, outsiders seem to have lost in this field to a more limited extent compared to the development described earlier for unemployment benefit. This indicates that deservingness and related perceptions still play a role – a discussion to be continued in the next section.

Due to different ways of quarantining mobile workers, migrants' delayed entitlement to access benefits can be argued to have kept changes more limited overall (Kramer et al, 2018), at least in the Netherlands and Denmark, as these rules did not allow for many to use the benefits. Overall, the data do not indicate strong retrenchment as the replacement rates have been changed only to a limited extent, although within the field of unemployment benefit for the long-term unemployed, gradual erosion can be witnessed in some countries, and some reduction can also be witnessed within the pension system.

Health, old age and family spending – a story of deservingness?

This section discusses whether there has been a development whereby the areas often seen as more deserving, not only in Europe, but also in the US (on health care, see Jensen and Petersen, 2017), have changed. Focus is also on these areas as, in general, they are popular areas among voters, as also argued earlier (Taylor-Gooby and Leruth, 2018). Table 5.10 shows the development in spending on old age as a percentage of GDP.

Table 5.10 is a strong indicator that there has been an increase in spending on old age. This can partly be explained by demographic change leading to increased numbers of elderly, but also because this area seems less likely to be hit by retrenchment (as argued in Chapter 2 and returned to several times throughout the book) as the elderly are a group seen as deserving, as well as a large voter group. Despite many pension reforms around the world (Bonoli and Shinkawa, 2005),

Table 5.10: Spending on social protection on old age as percentages of GDP in selected EU member states, 2006–15

GEO/TIME	2006	2008	2010	2012	2014	2015
Nordic:						
Denmark	10.5	10.3	11.1	11.3	11.8	11.6
Sweden	10.5	10.8	11.4	12.0	12.2	12.0
Continental:						
Germany	9.3	9.0	9.4	9.1	9.0	9.1
France	10.8	11.2	12.1	12.6	12.9	12.8
Liberal:						
Ireland	4.2	4.9	6.7	6.8	6.1	4.7
UK	9.6	10.4	11.7	12.1	11.6	11.6
Southern Europe:						
Spain	6.3	6.9	8.1	9.1	9.8	9.7
Italy	12.6	12.6	13.7	14.0	14.1	14.1
Eastern Europe:						
Czech Republic	6.5	7.0	8.1	8.8	8.4	8.1
Poland	9.3	8.9	9.1	9.0	9.3	–

Source: EUROSTAT, spr_exp_sum (accessed 13 August 2018)

the increase has slowed down in recent years (OECD, 2017). There are differences across welfare states; in Southern Europe, for example, spending on old age is around half of total social protection spending. Despite pension reforms, in other countries (Hinrichs, 2019), it has been a spending area where retrenchment has been less likely than other parts of the welfare state as a consequence of strong electoral support for welfare to the deserving elderly.

Table 5.11 takes a closer look at the level of spending on health and sickness, which is not only often a field with a high level of public support, but also an area with a high degree of universality in most countries.

The table reveals several interesting aspects, one being that Continental welfare states and the UK seem to be the high spenders in this field. Further, overall, the difference among countries besides that is only limited, albeit with Poland and Ireland lagging behind in the level of spending. Lastly, there seems to have been retrenchment in the field only to a more limited extent, albeit that a fixed percentage of GDP can cause a reduced amount of money to be available in times of reductions in GDP, especially given the demographic transitions taking place, with increasing numbers of elderly who might be in need of health care. The development of new medicines and types of treatment that help to ensure longer life expectancy might also be

Table 5.11: Spending on social protection on sickness and health as percentages of GDP in selected EU member states, 2006–15

GEO/TIME	2006	2008	2010	2012	2014	2015
Nordic:						
Denmark	6.0	6.2	6.7	6.5	6.3	6.3
Sweden	7.4	7.1	7.0	7.3	7.5	7.5
Continental:						
Germany	7.7	8.0	9.2	9.3	9.7	9.7
France	8.5	8.4	8.9	9.0	9.1	9.1
Liberal:						
Ireland	6.1	7.1	7.6	7.4	6.6	5.0
UK	7.3	7.3	8.3	8.7	8.4	9.9
Southern Europe:						
Spain	6.2	6.6	7.0	6.6	6.5	6.6
Italy	6.6	6.7	7.0	6.8	6.8	6.6
Eastern Europe:						
Czech Republic	5.7	5.5	6.0	6.0	6.0	5.8
Poland	3.8	4.4	4.4	4.1	4.0	–

Source: EUROSTAT, spr_exp_sum (accessed 13 August 2018)

a pressure in some countries. Still, overall, it seems to indicate that this is not a field with strong changes in welfare state spending and therefore no tendencies to retrenchment even in times of austerity, thereby implicitly showing that this is an area with seemingly high support from voters.

However, as argued earlier, it is important to look at the amount of money available in relation to the group possibly in need of care. Table 5.12 shows this for spending in relation to old age.

Table 5.12 shows very strong variation in the development of spending on old age, ranging from a strong increase in Ireland, Spain and Poland, as well as in the Czech Republic, the UK, France and Sweden, to a decline in Italy and Denmark. Per elderly person, the overall level is still highest in the Nordic welfare states. This development reflects changes in both the pension system and services within LTC. As argued earlier in this chapter (see also Greve, 2017), trends towards the use of re-enablement, rehabilitation, prevention and welfare technology might explain the development towards less spending on LTC. Healthier elderly people could also help in explaining the development, although one should then have expected a more common development across countries, unless some used new approaches to a greater extent than others. Naturally, this also reflects

Table 5.12: Spending in euros at constant 2010 prices on old age per inhabitant above the age of 65 since 2006 in selected EU member states

GEO/TIME	2006	2008	2010	2012	2014	2015	Change 2006–15
EU28	*	14,970	15,650	15,697	15,479	*	3.4%
Czech Republic	6,773	7,490	7,949	7,970	7,375	7,341	8.4%
Denmark	31,293	30,512	29,974	28,807	29,197	28,489	−6.7%
Germany	14,768	14,314	14,347	14,584	14,712	15,077	2.1%
Ireland	16,277	17,672	21,989	21,390	19,686	19,441	20.9%
Spain	9,406	10,367	11,267	11,060	11,339	11,462	20.6%
France	20,294	21,406	22,604	22,799	22,468	22,155	9.2%
Italy	18,045	17,518	18,216	17,549	16,634	16,726	−7.3%
Poland	5,577	5,906	6,414	6,381	6,500	*	16.6%
Sweden	23,666	24,561	24,804	25,186	25,199	25,536	7.9%
UK	18,533	20,043	21,142	21,193	20,308	20,313	9.6%

Notes: Naturally, given the increasing number of elderly able to take care of themselves and in good health, it can be debated whether the age group should have been different; however, as the data also include pensions, which are a central component related to old age in many countries, this choice of age group seems relevant. * = data not available.

Source: Calculated based upon Eurostat ESSPROS (European system of integrated social protection statistics) data and demographics

the fact that even before this increase in longevity and healthy life-years, in some countries, LTC has only had a more limited impact on the overall level of spending. Development in the pension system also influences the development; in Denmark, for example, occupational-based pensions seem to have developed strongly in this period, which has influenced welfare state spending in the area (Greve, 2018b). Besides the development in Italy and Denmark, the data indicate that spending has not been reduced in an area where voters seem to find that those in need are deserving, thus confirming that perceptions of needs can impact development. In contrast, Table 5.13 shows the development in spending on family and children in fixed prices and purchasing power parities (PPP)[5] for 2006–14.

The table is interesting in two respects. The first is the strong expansion of spending per child in Germany and Poland since the crisis, with a standstill in the other countries and retrenchment in the Czech Republic. For the UK, there was a strong increase from 2006 to 2008, but thereafter a standstill, albeit a reduction since 2010. The other is the clear deviation with Eastern and Southern Europe spending relatively limited amounts on family and children per child compared to the other countries. This might have a repercussion on the understanding of what government responsibilities are in different welfare regimes (see further in Chapter 7).

Financing welfare states

One issue that has been used as an argument for reductions in spending has been the difficulty of financing welfare states in the wake of the financial crisis, as well as international tax competition, especially in relation to how to finance welfare spending. The lowering of taxation on companies has been a trend for a long time. Albeit only an indicator of the overall development in the level of taxes and duties in the selected EU member states, the focus here is on the aggregate level of taxes and duties as a percentage of GDP (see Table 5.14) as this can also be an indicator of the state's willingness to provide welfare benefits and services.

Ireland has reduced taxes and duties dramatically over the period in consideration, whereas there have been standstills or even slight increases in other countries. Thus, the table does not lend support to the fact that, overall, cuts in taxes and duties have been on the agenda in most countries; therefore, the ambition of curbing welfare states by lowering taxes and duties has not been strongly on the agenda either. As Chapter 3 showed, this does not necessarily imply that

Table 5.13: Spending in euros in PPP per child (0–5 years) for family and children as social investment in selected EU member states

	2006	2007	2008	2009	2010	2011	2012	2013	2014
Czech Republic	6,061	7,277	7,320	6,809	6,343	5,769	5,560	5,651	5,585
Denmark	14,787	15,360	15,670	16,242	16,200	15,448	15,461	15,720	15,982
Germany	17,303	17,597	18,220	19,658	20,815	20,908	21,247	21,714	22,154
Spain	4,243	4,292	4,304	4,634	4,567	4,520	4,256	4,346	4,430
France	9,240	9,354	9,222	9,435	9,339	9,280	9,454	9,629	9,842
Ireland	7,634	7,955	8,296	8,777	9,767	9,111	8,685	8,115	7,918
Italy	2,990	3,258	3,332	3,401	3,331	3,286	3,249	3,240	3,234
Poland	1,821	1,947	3,096	3,162	3,216	3,126	3,419	3,694	4,366
Sweden	11,539	11,270	11,323	11,149	11,112	11,103	11,285	11,516	11,679
UK	8,731	9,589	10,047	10,810	11,500	11,430	11,233	10,675	10,636

Note: Includes family in-kind, family allowances and family leave expenditures.

Source: Ronchi (2016) (accessed 29 January 2018)

Table 5.14: Taxes and duties as percentages of GDP since 2006 in selected EU member states

GEO/TIME	2008	2010	2012	2014	2016	2017
EU28	43.7	43.5	44.7	45.0	44.7	44.9
Czech Republic	38.7	39.3	40.5	40.3	40.2	40.4
Denmark	53.6	54.0	54.5	56.4	53.2	52.9
Germany	43.4	43.0	44.3	44.6	45.0	45.2
Ireland	34.9	33.0	33.9	33.9	26.6	25.7
Spain	36.7	36.2	37.6	38.9	37.7	37.9
France	50.0	50.0	52.1	53.3	53.2	53.9
Italy	45.2	45.7	47.9	47.9	46.9	46.6
Poland	40.7	38.5	39.1	38.6	38.8	39.6
Sweden	52.0	50.8	50.4	49.6	50.6	50.3
UK	39.4	38.4	37.8	37.7	38.6	39.1

Source: EUROSTAT, gov_10a_main (accessed 15 August 2018)

inequality has remained the same as it has been on the rise. Still, this is a further indication that, overall, austerity and retrenchment need not have been the case in all parts of the welfare state. Naturally, part of the explanation also lies in the fact that many welfare states had a public sector deficit after the financial crisis, making it more difficult to change the level of taxes and duties. Overall, it is known that if taxes are increased on labour compared to capital, this will increase the degree of inequality; therefore, not only is the overall level of taxes and duties important, but the mix and combinations of different kinds of taxes and duties also have an impact (for a recent article, see Iosifidi and Mylonidis, 2017).

Conclusion

Overall, the development does not lend support to a strong thesis on retrenchment in welfare benefits or overall spending on social policy and social security in most welfare states in Europe since the financial crisis. Naturally, there are variations among countries and in different fields, implying that a general picture of austerity cannot be found since 2006 – and looking back further to the beginning of this century, the picture is the same. Perhaps this is due to the fact that public opinion, in general, does not support it (Taylor-Gooby and Leruth, 2018).

In line with expectations for priorities related to who does and does not deserve, there seems to be a stronger focus on elderly care and health care, and less so on labour market services and benefits. This in line with a welfare chauvinist approach. There might be different historical reasons for national development; however, it seems not to be the case that austerity is the only game in town. Demographic development does, however, influence the development, but even when taking into consideration spending on old age and family, the data do not support a general attempt at retrenchment. In fact, the replacement rate for pensioners is still high for those with low incomes. They have presumably often been in a more precarious situation in the labour market, with stagnant real wage development. Part of the pension reform around Europe might reduce this in the years to come, but how this then influences depends, in particular, on occupational welfare, which has not been included here. In the pension field especially, there is an important lack of information on this; as such, public coverage might not be a good indicator when comparing both countries and change over time (Grødem et al, 2018). Also, in the unemployment insurance system, occupational welfare might influence coverage in case of unemployment (Ozkan, 2014).

The fact that the development in spending for those using the welfare system is felt as retrenchment might partly be ascribed to, first, there being both fixed and flexible costs as one issue. Second, even if spending increases, more people might be in need of support, or new types of activities are covered by the same amount or only slightly more. This can be very difficult to depict. Third, there might have been adaptation to the level of spending, implying that voters want more than the current level.

Still, the development in spending indicates that the perception of who deserves can be a reason for the development in specific parts of the welfare state. Populist support for these groups, where migrants are not the main group of beneficiaries, also lends support for welfare state development with a strong focus on natives as recipients of support. Thus, populism, both right and left, can imply support for welfare state development in a direction with a strong focus in line with a welfare chauvinistic approach. At the same time, this indicates that retrenchment does not necessarily take place in all sectors and all countries. Instead, there seem to be a continuous development of welfare states. Prioritising might thus imply that retrenchment takes place for some groups in order to pay for welfare to the elderly and health care.

Notes

[1] Occupational welfare can further have an impact; see the special issue of *Social Policy & Administration* (2018), 52(2).

[2] Naturally, this also implies that if further studies use 2010 as a starting point, the conclusion, albeit misleading, might indicate austerity. The choice of the starting year for analysis is thereby important.

[3] This is based upon Annex B in Langenbucher (2015), in which 11 different items related to eligibility and unemployment benefits and their development since 2011 are shown.

[4] The impact of reforms can be difficult to measure as it often takes many years before they are fully implemented, and changes in the pension system might be connected to changes in the tax system, making the reason for the precise impact less clear for voters.

[5] One can question the use of PPP for looking into the development; however, for the purpose here, this is less of a problem as the idea is to paint a picture by taking into consideration the group considered in need of support, in this case, the 0–5 age group.

References

Adema, W. and Ladaique, M. (2009) *How expensive is the welfare state? Gross and net indicators in the OECD Social Expenditure Database (SOCX).* Paris: OECD.

Aspinal, F., Glasby, J., Rostgaard, T., Tuntland, H.K., Westendorp, R. (2016) New horizons: reablement – supporting older people towards independence. *Age and Ageing*, O: 1–5.

Avent, R. (2017) *The wealth of humans: Work and its absence in the twenty-first century*. London: Penguin Books.

Bolukbasi, H. and Öktem, K. (2018) Conceptualizing and operationalizing social rights: towards higher convergent validity in SCIP and CWED. *Journal of European Social Policy*, 8(1): 86–100.

Bonoli, G. (2010) The political economy of active labour market policy. REC-WP 01/2010, Working Papers on the Reconciliation of Work and Welfare in Europe (Recwowe), Edinburgh, Dissemination and Dialogue Centre.

Bonoli, G. and Shinkawa, T. (2005) *Ageing and pension reform around the world: Evidence from eleven countries*. Cheltenham: Edward Elgar.

Clasen, J., Clegg, D. and Goerne, A. (2016) Comparative social policy analysis and active labour market policy: putting quality before quantity. *Journal of Social Policy*, 45(1): 21–38.

Dean, H. (2007) The ethics of welfare-to-work. *Policy & Politics*, 35(4): 573–89.

Emmenegger, P., Häusermann, S., Palier, B. and Seeleib-Kaiser, M. (eds) (2012) *The age of dualization: The changing face of inequality in deindustrialization societies*. Oxford: Oxford University Press.

Ervik, R., Kildal, N. and Nilssen, E. (eds) (2015) *New contractualism in European welfare state policies*. Oxford: Ashgate.

Greve, B. (2014) Occupational and fiscal welfare in times of crisis. In K. Farnsworth, Z. Irving and M. Fenger (eds) *Social policy review 26: Analysis and debate in social policy 2014*. Bristol: Policy Press.

Greve, B. (ed) (2017) *Long-term care for the elderly in Europe*. Oxon: Routledge.

Greve, B. (2018a) Long-term care. In B. Greve (ed) *The Routledge handbook of the welfare state* (2nd edn). Oxon: Routledge.

Greve, B. (2018b) At the heart of the Nordic occupational welfare model: Occupational welfare trajectories in Sweden and Denmark. *Social Policy & Administration*, 52(2): 508–18.

Greve, B. (ed) (2019) *The Routledge handbook of the welfare state* (2nd edn). Oxon: Routledge.

Grødem, A., Hagelund, J. and Hippe, J. (2018) Beyond coverage: the politics of occupational pension and the role of trade unions. Introduction to special issue. *Transfer*, 24(1): 9–23.

Hinrichs, K. (2019) Old age and pensions. In B. Greve (ed) *The Routledge handbook of the welfare state* (2nd edn). Oxon: Routledge.

Iosifidi, M. and Mylonidis, N. (2017) Relative effective taxation and income inequality: evidence from OECD countries. *Journal of European Social Policy*, 27(1): 57–76.

Jahn, D. (2017) Distribution regimes and redistribution effects during retrenchment and crisis: a *cui bono* analysis of unemployment replacement rates of various income categories in 31 welfare states. *Journal of European Social Policy*, 28(5): 433–51.

Jensen, C. and Petersen, M. (2017) The deservingness heuristic and the politics of health care. *American Journal of Political Science*, 61(1): 68–83.

Jensen, C., Arndt, C., Lee, S. and Wenzelburger, G. (2018) Policy instruments and welfare state reform. *Journal of European Social Policy*, 28(2): 161–76.

Jessourla, M. (2015) The Jobs Act: balancing across-the-board labour market flexibility with increased security? ESPN – flash report, European Commission.

Kennet, P. and Lendvai-Baiton, N. (eds) (2017) *Handbook of European social policy*. Chelthenham: Edward Elgar.

Kramer, D., Thierry, J. and Van Hooren, F. (2018) Responding to free-movement: quarantining mobile union citizens in European welfare states. *Journal of European Public Policy*, 25(10): 1501–21.

Langenbucher, K. (2015) *How demanding are eligibility criteria for unemployment benefits, quantitative indicators for OECD and EU countries.* OECD Social, Employment and Migration Working Papers, No. 166, Paris: OECD.

Marchal, S. and Marx, I. (2018) Stemming the tide: what have European Countries done to support low-wage workers in an era of downward wage pressure? *Journal of European Social Policy*, 28(1): 18–33.

Meyer, T. (2017) How European pension promises changed in austere times. In P. Kennet and N. Lendvai-Baiton (eds) *Handbook of European social policy*. Chelthenham: Edward Elgar.

Midgley, J., Dahl, E. and Wright, A. (ed) (2017) *Social investment and social welfare: International and critical perspectives*. Cheltenham: Edward Elgar.

Morel, N., Palier, B. and Palme J. (ed) (2012) *Towards a social investment welfare state: Ideas, policies and challenges*. Bristol: Policy Press.

OECD (Organisation for Economic Co-operation and Development) (2017) *Pensions at a glance*. Paris: OECD.

Ozkan, U. (2014) Comparing formal unemployment compensation systems in 15 OECD countries. *Social Policy & Administration*, 48(1): 44–66.

Ronchi, S. (2016) The Social Investment Welfare Expenditure data set (SIWE): a new methodology for measuring the progress of social investment in EU welfare state budget. GK-SOCLIFE, Working Paper Series, 16-2016.

Ronchi, S. (2018) Which roads (if any) to social investment? The recalibration of EU welfare states at the crisis crossroads (2000–2014). *Journal of Social Policy*, pp 1–20, DOI: 10.1017/S0047279417000782.

Roth, L., Afonso, A. and Spies, D. (2018) The impact of populist Radical Right parties on socio-economic policies. *European Political Science Review*, 10(3): 325–50.

Saxonberg, S. and Sirovátka, T. (2009) Neo-liberalism by decay? The evolution of the Czech welfare state. *Social Policy & Administration*, 43: 186–203.

Taylor-Gooby, P. and Leruth, B. (ed) (2018) *Attitudes, aspirations and welfare. Social policy directions in uncertain times*. Cham: Palgrave Macmillan.

Taylor-Gooby, P., Leruth, B. and Chung, H. (eds) (2017) *After austerity: Welfare state transformation in Europe after the Great Recession*. Oxford: Oxford University Press.

Wang, J. and Vliet, O. (2016) Social assistance and minimum income benefits: benefit levels, replacement rates and policies across 26 OECD countries, 1990–2009. *European Journal of Social Security*, 18(4): 333–55.

Watts, B. and Fitzpatrick, S. (2018) *Welfare conditionality*. Oxon: Routledge.

Wiles, J., Leibing, A., Guberman, N., Reeve, J., Allen, R.E.S. (2012) The meaning of 'aging in place' to older people. *The Gerontologist*, 52(3): 357–66.

6

Has social cohesion been eroded?

Introduction

So far, the book has revolved around concepts and mainly quantitative data, information and analysis on central aspects of welfare state development. This chapter looks into stories about people's perceptions of welfare state developments and why they do not trust the political system and the administration, or what is often labelled the 'elite'. The chapter draws on a number of recent books and articles trying to depict and understand people's opinions – from Brexit to the vote for Trump – where one might witness a contradiction between possible self-interest and support for populist viewpoints (such as Putnam, 2015; Hochschild, 2016; Vance, 2016; Winlow et al, 2017). However, this applies not only to 'ordinary' voters, but also to politicians, such as what happened in the British Brexit debate with arguments of the threat from immigration (Romano, 2018); thus, perceptions can be influenced in different ways. The attempt is to systematise why, in particular, groups with low incomes and having a precarious position in the labour market (if having a job at all) vote for populist and/or liberal policies that might not, at the end of the day, improve their standard of living. The possible distance between 'them and us' as a theme is also included. Conceptual issues related to social capital and social cohesion are a common thread throughout the chapter as there is also a need for identity (Sen, 2007), and the lack thereof might influence behaviour.

The next section extracts information from the books mentioned earlier, and includes a few others as well. One weakness is that several of the books deal with the development in the US; however, there is no indication that the same tendencies or reasons for the US development will not also prevail in Europe, as clarified by the end of the chapter and shown in examples for other countries.

In the next section, the focus is on two areas in the US where there can be argued to be a cleavage between the perception and understanding of societal development, and the fact that what the 'elite' sees as important is very prevalent. This is followed by a discussion of the possible erosion of social capital by continuously more segregated societies, including Putnam's depiction of the change of social connectedness. Then, the next section moves towards a presentation of the dark side of some extreme approaches, attempting to link this to populism and welfare chauvinism, as defined and discussed in Chapter 2. Finally, the attempt in the last section is to sum up what this might inform us about and how it helps in explaining the possible erosion of trust and support for welfare state development, including how the 'them and us' debate might influence perceptions of the role of the state.

'Hillbilly' and 'strangers in their own land' – why?

Hillbilly elegy (Vance, 2016) is the story of families with a hope that every new generation would have more and better options than the previous generation, and it is also a personal story about how families in the US moving from Kentucky's Appalachia region to Ohio after the Second World War had exactly that hope. *Strangers in their own land* (Hochschild, 2016) tells the story of Louisiana based upon qualitative interviews and looking for in-depth stories in an area where the Tea Party is strong.[1] The stories in the books are also about changed class relations and change in hopes and expectations for the future.

Already, in the opening chapter of *Strangers*, there is the following quote: 'When I was a kid, you stuck a thumb out by the side of the road, you got a ride. Or if you had a car, you gave a ride. If someone was hungry, you fed him. You had community. You know what's undercut all that? He pauses. "Big government"' (Hochschild, 2016: 4). This illustrates a by-now deep-seated mistrust in the government, and thereby also an indirect mistrust in suggestions that would attempt to support local development by government initiatives. There are several quotes indicating the negative attitude towards the government, which is also seen being too big and too ineffective, which show that if they could get local development with a stronger focus on the local community, they would prefer this. Also evident from these studies is the belief that global economic and political development is negative for their life chances or is more or less non-existent. This illustrates a gap between the elite, who believe in global trade and global interaction, and people's everyday life in areas where there are few jobs and low income, as well as an understanding that globalisation is seen as a scapegoat, besides government, for the development and their lack of options.

In the US, republican states are 'poorer and have more teen mothers, more divorce, worse health, more obesity, more trauma-related deaths, more low-birth-weight babies and lower school enrolment' (Hochschild, 2016: 8), as well as lower life expectancy. Therefore, one should expect that they would be likely to support the development of state support for more welfare; however, as also indicated by the earlier quote, this is not the case despite many, in fact, using the services available.

Therefore, despite, in many ways, Louisiana being in need of state support to cope with pollution, to create jobs and to ensure a decent standard of living, there is a clear majority who believe that it would be better without the government and the 'elite' running the system, which they do for their own interests only, in Washington. In this case, and as is often the case in Europe, the 'them and us' theme is not, at the outset, related to migrants and others who can be used as scapegoats; rather, the situation here is more to do with criticism of the existing political system, in which there is a lack of trust. This is despite the fact that migrants do not, as sometimes argued, expect more from welfare states than natives do (Lubbers et al, 2018). Therefore, as is often the case, seeing them as a burden on welfare states is not necessarily logical.

Here, there is a combination of three central issues for people: taxes, faith and honour. Hochschild's description of the development of pollution and the impact on local society, including the possibility of fishing, has seemingly had the opposite view to asking for more regulation: 'I think they overregulate the bottom because it's harder to regulate the top' (Hochschild, 2016: 52); 'the state always seems to come down on the little guy' (Hochschild, 2016: 52); or, even sharper, 'I hate the word "regulate"' (Hochschild, 2016: 122). This also implies that despite many in these geographical areas being in need of support, there is a strong feeling that non-working, undeserving people get too much, and this influences the level of tax paid by those having a job, but also the honour of being a hard-working person.

It is also a story about the fact that all the attempts to ensure equal treatment, avoiding discrimination and helping in equal opportunities regardless of sex, religion, race and sexual preferences have had the opposite impact on many white middle- or lower-class people, as argued: 'Blacks, women, immigrants, refugees, brown pelicans – all have cut ahead of you in line. But it's people like you who have made this country great' (Hochschild, 2016: 139). To put it another way, the attempt to ensure fair treatment and rights for all has implied a criticism of central authorities as some people have found that they are not respected, and their values and contributions are set back by spending time and money on other groups. This can also fit with the fact that there has been a decline in the number of jobs and wage income for many white-collar workers. Thus, a growing divide between the establishment (or what is often labelled the 'elite') and the anti-establishment (or what is often labelled the 'populist') is a stronger and more obvious dividing line than those who have influenced the development and support for various anti-elitist groups. It is also a story about the decline in what people believed in: the lack of jobs and a society with equality not only in relation to the classical economic form, but also in the options and hope for the future.

In many ways, Vance's description of his own upbringing and development is a story of the same understanding among parts of the population as Hoschschild's (2016), while, at the same time, pointing to the fact that there are sometimes people who, in one way or another, are able to support a person and make social mobility happen, in this case, his grandmother. It is also a story about change in societies impacting different groups differently:

> When the factories shut their doors, the people left behind were trapped in towns and cities that could no longer support such large populations with high-quality work. Those who could – generally the well educated, wealthy, or well connected – left, leaving behind communities of poor people. (Vance, 2016: 144)

This reminds us that this is why globalisation and the constant search for more effective ways of producing goods and services also cause many low-skilled people to lose out; therefore, they do not buy into the idea of globalisation as they see it is as representing something being taken away from them, as well as their hopes and dreams for the future.

The same picture emerges in other studies and interviews. These include references to others arguing about what we could today see as being versions of 'them and us' and/or perceiving that some are receiving benefits that they do not deserve: 'I vote republican because I'm against other people (authority figures) taking my money (that I work hard for) and giving it to a non-producing, welfare collecting, single mother, crack baby producing future democrat' (Haidt, 2013: 195).

It is argued that a possible reason for the split in viewpoints could be that leftist-leaning fairness causes equality, whereas 'on the right it means proportionality – people should be rewarded in proportion to what they contribute, even if that guarantees unequal outcome' (Haidt, 2013: 161). This is not only in the US as the Conservatives in the UK have argued for cuts in benefits for those who do not want to work, and we have seen a tightening towards a work-first approach in many welfare states (see Chapter 5).

Additionally, the history and belief that the US's role was central in the Second World War (as it was) also implies that for many, including Vance's grandmother, they have 'two gods: Jesus Christ and the United States' (Vance, 2016: 189), and this trust in both the country and local community has been weakened by developments in recent years. The change has seemingly implied that 'there is a cultural movement in the white working class to blame problems on society or the government, and that movement gains adherents by the day' (Vance, 2016: 195). The change in culture and mistrust in institutions is also prevalent in Vance's family, where his father asked him whether he had 'pretended to be black or liberal' (Vance, 2016: 194) in order to be enrolled at Yale Law School as a student. This mistrust in fairness and, in fact, the equal rights development that has been part of the fight in many affluent countries has, in this sense, been turned upside down, with the belief that others get what they themselves are not able to get. Furthermore, a problem is that the ability to ensure social movement across generations has been diminishing overall in recent years, thus causing a divide in the US – and also in Europe – that influences policy development and options for more populist, often right-wing, parties to succeed.

Social capital's erosion

Although social capital is difficult to measure, and there might be a strong variation in the understanding of the conceptual issues (for an overview, see Halpern, 2005), social capital has been an important issue since it was introduced (Coleman, 1988). Furthermore, since Putnam's (2001) *Bowling alone*, there has been strong interest in the topic as this relates to aspects such as trust and social cohesion. The possible impact of welfare chauvinism and populism could be a further erosion of trust and social connectedness, especially as increased inequality, as depicted in Chapter 3, can make social networks shrink, and thereby also influence the situation of poor people the most (Christoforous and Davis, 2014).

Thus, if information is available indicating that segregation has increased, this also implies that social connections and social capital in societies have been reduced. This is, in fact, the case, as described and analysed in Putnam's (2015) book. It is on this book that the following discussion is mainly based as it shows that opportunities for different groups in US society have widened, meaning that some young people have far more options than other young people, or, to put it another way, social mobility has been reduced in the US. Moreover, this is in the wake of an 'unprecedented growth in inequality in America' (Putnam, 2015: 36), as also in Europe (see Chapter 3).

Due to the increase in inequality, there has also been increased educational and neighbourhood segregation. As described in the book, 50 years ago, the rich and the poor lived together in the same area. Gated communities were few and children attended the same schools. At the same time, a collapse of the working class started more than 30 years ago, and 'the wages of the men without college degrees have fallen since the early 1970's' (Putnam, 2015: 73), causing a still more diversified society where there are no longer options available for all persons to move up the ladder. This reduced social mobility (as depicted in Chapter 2) is clearly witnessed by some of the population as a consequence of changes in the labour market, new technology and so on, making them reluctant to support those political parties that have supported this type of development in the past.

In the local area where Putnam interviewed people, differences in society were revealed, including the fact that in one area, 30% of the young aged between 16 and 24 were not in school and did not have a job, whereas in a more affluent area, the number was only 3%. Thereby, opportunities to move across and use options are very different. Moreover, those coming from more affluent areas participated to a higher degree in extracurricular activities, and in those areas, 'non-cognitive skills and habits such as grit, teamwork, and sociability are unmistakably developed among participants in extracurricular activities' (Putnam, 2015: 176).

Differences in neighbourhood, upbringing and options influence individuals' opportunities and perceptions thereof. Naturally, as also argued in the book, the link from income inequality to inequality in opportunity is not clear-cut. However, as Putnam (2015: 228) writes:

> it took several decades for economic malaise to undermine family structures and community support. It took several decades for gaps in parenting and schooling to develop; and it will take decades more for the full impact of those divergent childhood influences to manifest themselves in adult lives.

This implies that the growth in inequality in the US (see Chapter 3) has had a profound impact on other aspects of society. With the growing inequality in Europe, this is likely to also have these detrimental impacts in various European countries. Lastly, the implication of this reduction in social mobility is also lower economic growth as more people do not get the necessary qualifications that should enable them to participate in new developments and new options in the labour market.

The dark side and populist movements

With growing discontent, there is naturally the risk that some who feel they have nothing to lose might want more and are willing to support political parties arguing for changes that are more dramatic. This can reflect lost opportunities, low income or dire poverty, but also feelings about the fact that others have been moved forward in the queue, such as the example mentioned earlier. This can be across culture and religion, but if others perceive themselves as being 'demoted from the center of their country's consciousness to it fringe' (Justin, 2016: 15), then this explains part of their resentment and willingness to support more populism, and even more dramatic aspects. Among other things, this can be witnessed on the dark net (Bartlett, 2015), where all sorts of issues, most of which are illegal, are discussed.

The changed role of the working class in the UK has given rise to, and influenced, Brexit, but also a sense of feeling deprived of opportunities. All the plus-words arising from both third way politics, such as 'extended choice' and 'competition' (Powell, 2013), and improved welfare services, while embracing the market's opportunities and a global agenda, were not seen as positive by those in areas where industrial jobs were in plentiful supply 20 years ago. To put it another way:

> Where was the freedom for the retail worker struggling by on a zero-hours contract.... And exactly where was this choice they heard so much about? They didn't choose to be downwardly mobile. They didn't choose to be surrounded by wave after wave of new economic competitors. They didn't choose multiculturalism. (Winlow et al, 2017: 120)

Thus, those losing out from the development thought that they were promised something that they did not get. Instead, they have a feeling that they have been left out.

In the English Defence League (EDL), this has led to criticism of migrants, often seeing Muslims as those who are the reason why they do not have options, as one has said:

> Where I live, they [Muslims] are the ones with the nice cars, the big houses, their kids running round like jack the lads in Mercs and Beemers [Mercedes and BMW cars] that have been bought by ripping us off in their shops for a pint of milk while they look after their own. (Winlow et al, 2017: 155)

As put in another study in relation not only to the position of migrants, but also more broadly to receiving benefits: 'the people who are trying to get away from war and then you've got the economic refugees who haven't really got a reason for leaving where they live except they want to get some more money' (Taylor-Gooby et al, 2018: 920). Another quote from the same study indicates that there is an idea that money spent on migrants can have a negative impact on other parts of the welfare state: 'I think you allow immigration more and more and more, the Government have to spend more money on benefits for them instead of putting the money into education and social care and other kind of stuff' (Taylor-Gooby et al, 2018: 920). Therefore, in this way, the search for a scapegoat has found a face that can be used to explain why certain groups do not have the options that they would like to have, or expected to have. Thus, strong attitudes and approaches also seem to be justified as a reaction to lost opportunities.

Many of those who supported the UK Independence Party (UKIP) in the UK were also those who supported the EDL, although not always doing it openly and despite the fact that they were also not aware of UKIP's 'commitment to the neo-liberal model or its desire to shrink the welfare state' (Winlow et al, 2017: 148). Therefore, again, this contradicts what might be beneficial or in the self-interest of a group, which is often seen as an issue in relation to legitimacy (see Chapter 2). This contradiction between aims, policies and ideas might be a useful reference when considering why there can be negative approaches to and understandings of how, what is considered to be, the 'establishment' acts. In this way, it is argued that the political Left, with its commitment to 'equality, security and common ownership' (Winlow et al, 2017: 150), was not seen as legitimate among those who, instead, saw that others took their jobs and so on, and thus, in many ways, no longer supported solidarity; rather, 'in the absence of an explanation rooted in political economy the EDL have identified

Muslims as the objective cause of their frustration and anxiety' (Winlow et al, 2017: 154).

Furthermore, members of the EDL feel that they have had to wait for housing or for jobs, but that it has been too easy for Muslims, who are then used as a scapegoat for the development. In the eyes of EDL supporters, they 'are obviously just playing the system' (Winlow et al, 2017: 161); in other words, they are not seen as deserving of support from the welfare state.

Overall, 'the reality is that supporters of the EDL dream of returning to a mythical time in which everything "just seemed to work"' (Winlow et al, 2017: 170). In this way, the dream of a better world argued by some as would be the case by increasing globalisation and free trade was not seen by these groups: they do not feel that they have gained from international – or even national – development. Therefore, the consequence of anxiety about the future and having lost the dream of a better world is the risk of having negative feelings. To put it another way, the culture that they grew up in has vanished, with no prospect of a dream to believe in for the future.

Part of this also reflects the debate on what, in fact, European culture is, and with particular reference to the EU's political class: 'according to its anti-populist cultural script, nationalism is the natural companion of xenophobia' (Furedi, 2018: 15). This also indicates a conflict between those gaining from international development and those losing, who see nationalism and national politics as in contrast to a cosmopolitan culture, as is also the case in many European countries. Given that social ties are important for development, it is also important to ensure not only that are economic issues included, but also that social norms are important (Pentland, 2015).

However, support for the welfare state can also be witnessed, for example, in the universalistic Nordic welfare states, which have an understanding of reciprocity in the welfare system. The argument for this, for example, is: 'Well it's sort of a foundation. Since we have a democratic society where we consider everyone to have equal worth, then we should secure basic comfort and security for everyone' (Man, 55, quoted in Frederiksen, 2018: 7). This idea of risk pooling can be seen in qualitative interviews, where it is seen as central 'that recipients contribute, have contributed or will contribute in the future, to the best of their ability' (Frederiksen, 2018: 9). Naturally, if some doubt whether this is actually the case, it could reduce support for welfare states, as well as legitimacy (see also Chapter 2).

Conclusion: what does this tell us?

The critique of public administration and mistrust in government was described early by Richard Nixon: 'The nine most terrifying words in the English language are: I'm from the government and I'm here to help' (cited in Klein, 2017: 80). Thus, if there is mistrust in the government's abilities to support individuals, especially as part of a right-wing liberal agenda of a stronger role for the market, then this is an idea that can influence voters' decisions to support populist parties. Lack of trust is a central issue (Taylor-Gooby et al, 2018).

In many countries, the dream of change and a better world, as well as support for Left politics (while different between countries), with a focus on solidarity and equality, has been challenged by the loss of jobs, low wage rises and increased pressure on the daily standard of living. Even in countries where the standard of living is still rising, as we compare ourselves with others, this can also cause an increase in the negative stance towards the elite, migrants and/or others who, in a variety of ways, are used as a scapegoat for a development where historical positions have been eroded. The need for identity thus seems to be a core aspect of why the in-depth stories presented in this chapter imply support for populist approaches and welfare chauvinist policies.

In this way, this also reflects the debate on the legitimacy of the welfare state (see Chapter 2) as it is not seen as legitimate that their way of life is not supported, whereas this is the case for many others. Thus, the policy towards equality and justice for groups that, over time, have had difficult positions due to their different racial, ethnic, sexual and/or religious position is seen as a threat to those who see themselves as hard-working and even as pushed back to a waiting position in relation to jobs, money, housing and so on. Thus, the fight to avoid discrimination and to ensure a more equal stance in societies has implied that part of the population feels alienated as a consequence.

Welfare state development building on a dream of opportunities for all has thus been weakened by both ideas (see Chapter 2) and a development where some groups feel left behind in the options for a better life, not only for themselves, but also for their children. Overall, the reduced social cohesion described in this chapter indicates why we see polarisation in societies, which, at the same time, builds towards a 'them and us' situation.

Note

[1] In the rest of this section, these two books are only referred to when using a direct quote from the books.

References

Bartlett, J. (2015) *The dark net*. London: Windmill Books.

Christoforous, A. and Davis, J. (eds) (2014) *Social capital and economics. Social values, power, and social identity*. Oxon: Routledge.

Coleman, J. (1988) Social capital in the creation of human capital. *Journal of Sociology*, 94: 95–120.

Frederiksen, M. (2018) Varieties of Scandinavian universalism: a comparative study of welfare justifications. *Acta Sociologica*, 61(1): 3–16.

Furedi, F. (2018) *Populism and the European culture wars: The conflict of values between Hungary and the EU*. Oxon: Routledge.

Haidt, J. (2013) *The righteous mind: Why good people are divided by politics and religion*. London: Penguin.

Halpern, D. (2005) *Social capital*. Cambridge: Polity.

Hochschild, A. (2016) *Strangers in their own land: Anger and mourning on the American Right*. New York, NY: The New Press.

Justin, G. (2016) *The new minority: White working class politics in an age of immigration and inequality*. Oxford: Oxford University Press.

Klein, N. (2017) *No is not enough: Defeating the new shock politics*. St. Ives: Allen Lane.

Lubbers, M., Diehl, C., Kuhn, T. and Larsen, C.A. (2018) Migrants' support for welfare state spending in Denmark, Germany and the Netherlands. *Social Policy & Administration*, 52(4): 895–913.

Pentland, A. (2015) *Social physics: How social networks can make us smarter*. New York, NY: Penguin Books.

Powell, M. (2013) Third Way. In B. Greve (ed) *The Routledge handbook of the welfare state*. Oxon: Routledge.

Putnam, R. (2001) *Bowling alone: The collapse and revival of American community*. New York, NY: Touchstone.

Putnam, R (2015) *Our kids: The American dream in crisis*. New York, NY: Simon and Schuster.

Romano, S. (2018) *Moralising poverty: The 'undeserving' poor in the public gaze*. Oxon: Routledge.

Sen, A. (2007) *Identity & violence: The illusion of destiny*. London: Penguin.

Taylor-Gooby, P., Chung, H. and Leruth, B. (2018) The contribution of deliberative forums to studying welfare state attitudes. *Social Policy & Administration*, 52(2): 914–27.

Vance, J.D. (2016) *Hillbilly elegy. A memoir of a family and culture in crisis*. London: William Collins.

Winlow, S., Hall, S. and Treadwell, J. (2017) *The rise of the Right. English nationalism and the transformation of working-class politics*. Bristol: Policy Press.

7

What do we know about citizens' perception of the welfare state?

Anders Ejrnæs and Bent Greve

Introduction

This chapter deals with citizens' (and thereby voters') perception of what welfare states should do and what they do not support, or at least support to a lesser degree, as the responsibilities of the welfare state, using several surveys and studies that have tried to depict this. This is done, first, in the second section, by presenting existing analysis, especially analysis based upon the European Social Survey (ESS) special rotating module in 2008. In the third section, the development is analysed by combining the special module in 2008 with the one in 2016, which is possible because 17 European countries took part in both surveys. As these countries also cover sufficiently large varieties of welfare regimes, it is possible to delve into whether the development has been different in various kinds of welfare state. In the fourth section, other data are presented that, in a variety of ways, provide evidence on support or not to the welfare state. The fifth section then sums up the analysis.

Earlier analysis

Naturally, there are pitfalls and risks from using different surveys as questions can be understood differently in different countries (Chung et al, 2018), but also because recent policy discussions and/or changes in one or more policy areas in a country might have had an impact on the viewpoints of citizens. Furthermore, a single event might influence perceptions, for example, on migrants, as seemingly happened with the refugee crisis in 2015/16. However, a survey is one of the best ways to obtain information, although new approaches are under way.[1] Still, in order to conduct comparative analysis, the use of a survey is a solid method, especially because several surveys have been repeated, making it possible to look into changes over time.

A core issue in the analysis of the ESS data for 2008 was to ask respondents about the government's responsibility to ensure:

1. a job for everyone who wants one;
2. adequate health care for the sick;
3. a reasonable standard of living for the old;
4. a reasonable standard of living for the unemployed;
5. sufficient childcare services for working parents; and
6. paid leave from work for people who temporarily have to care for sick family members.

Using a scale ranging from 0 (for not government's responsibility) to 10 (for entirely government's responsibility), an index can be constructed, which is shown in Table 7.1.

It is striking that, in 2008, it was countries in Eastern and Southern Europe where people wanted a higher responsibility for the government to intervene, while, at the same time, the deviation in viewpoints is stronger in these countries, indicating more split opinions on the role of the state. This can be due to different reasons:

- that the size of welfare states is seen as too small in those countries;
- that citizens in the Nordic and Continental countries find that there has already been too strong a development in government's responsibility; or
- that there is current provision of public childcare. (Chung and Meuleman, 2017)

It might further be due to the historical legacy and the long period of economic hardship in Eastern Europe (European Social Survey, 2012). The data thus point to a wish for welfare state intervention that varies given the size of the already-existing level of state intervention. This also implies that the legitimacy of the welfare state can be influenced by the already-existing size and structure, but naturally also by the welfare state's ability to help in solving prevailing problems – real or perceived. Causality might thus run, in some instances, in reverse order.

Another early analysis, albeit with data from 2002/03 and 2008/09 (ESS rounds 1 and 4), showed that 'people who are welfare chauvinist tend to be reluctant to support the welfare state' (Ervasti and Hjerm, 2012: 168). The development since then seems to indicate that this is not necessarily the case (see later in the chapter).

Table 7.1: Welfare index for European countries, 2008

Country	Mean	Standard deviation
Belgium	7.13	1.21
Bulgaria	8.32	1.62
Croatia	8.16	1.75
Cyprus	8.11	1.28
Czech Republic	7.34	1.77
Denmark	7.59	1.18
Estonia	7.92	1.55
Finland	7.84	1.13
France	7.05	1.41
Germany	7.35	1.54
Greece	8.65	1.41
Hungary	8.24	1.45
Israel	8.32	1.40
Latvia	8.83	1.40
Netherlands	6.77	1.13
Norway	7,86	1,19
Poland	7.73	1.59
Portugal	8.11	1.54
Romania	7.65	2.13
Russia	8.31	1.63
Slovakia	7.24	1.64
Slovenia	7.80	1.46
Spain	8.30	1.24
Sweden	7.74	1.29
Switzerland	6.43	1.56
Turkey	7.90	1.95
Ukraine	8.79	1.52
UK	7.22	1.33
Total	7.82	1.61

Note: Not all countries in the 2008 wave were included in the 2016 survey.
Source: Svallfors (2014)

Naturally, the average measure of answers to different questions related to responsibility can be due to a number of reasons. However, as a starting point for looking into changes, as well as into a development influenced by an external economic shock, such as the financial crisis, the average indicates an important variation, which is pursued in the next section.

A Swedish study thus 'found that an increasing share of immigrants leads to lower preferred level of social benefits' (Dahlberg et al, 2012).

Albeit that the data used are from 1985 to 1994, the results are in line with an understanding of welfare chauvinism. Overall, another recent study also indicated that support for right-wing populist parties was higher in rural regions and in areas with a high percentage of foreigners, but also with a high number of people with a university degree (Stockemer, 2017).

What has happened since 2008 to perceptions?

The interesting issue here is to look into whether there has been a change in the support for welfare states since 2008 and also whether this has been dependent on the type of welfare state. Furthermore, the section goes into some detail about whether the support for intervention varies across policy fields. It is not possible to replicate Table 7.1 as not all the same countries are involved and some of the questions are different, but it is possible to use data from the 2008 and 2016 surveys to look into actual issues, which then indicate the development.

The focus on the deservingness/undeservingness question is analysed by looking into the question of whether the unemployed are looking for work. The development of the viewpoints on this question is shown in Table 7.2.

Looking at the overall picture, there is thus no indication that the perception among citizens is negative as to whether the unemployed are actually trying to cheat the system. In fact, there has been a slight increase in those trusting the unemployed to search for a job, which might partially reflect the high level of unemployment as more people might know persons who are unemployed and actively searching for a job.

Table 7.2: Opinions on whether most unemployed people do not really try to find a job and change herein for countries in the ESS survey, 2008–16

	2008	2016
Agree strongly	8.2	7.8
Agree	29.6	28.8
Neither agree nor disagree	24.6	24.3
Disagree	32.3	32.6
Disagree strongly	5.3	6.4

Note: All countries are included in the survey, and thus might be influenced by change herein, but in order to get the broad picture, this is less of a problem.

Source: Based upon ESS welfare attitudes, 2008 and 2016

In order to measure the development in attitudes towards different welfare policies, the respondents who were covered in the ESS surveys of 2008 and 2016 were asked about the government's responsibility to ensure:

1. a reasonable standard of living for the old;
2. a reasonable standard of living for the unemployed; and
3. sufficient childcare services for working parents.

The scale ranges from 0 (for not government's responsibility) to 10 (for entirely government's responsibility).

Table 7.3 shows the mean values on the attitudes towards the three different policy areas. When it comes to childcare, the table shows that in 11 countries, support for governmental responsibility increased in the period from 2008 to 2016, which is in line with other studies (Chung and Meuleman, 2017), except for Finland, Spain and Hungary. The support for governmental responsibility when it comes to ensuring a reasonable standard of living for the unemployed and old, however, decreased over the time period in 11 countries for the unemployed and 16 out of 17 for the old. However, the table also shows that support for governmental responsibility is still the highest for ensuring a reasonable standard of living for the old, and the lowest for ensuring a reasonable standard of living for the unemployed, although declining in six, including two Nordic countries with already high levels of coverage. This is generally in line with the expectation of whom voters will support as the elderly, as argued earlier in the book, are seen as deserving and are also still mainly native, in line with the welfare chauvinism and self-interest argument. There are exceptions, however, with Germany and Slovenia having higher support for childcare, although the path towards higher spending in the field and the acceptance of this, in Germany at least, can help in explaining this.

Another interesting issue is that there is no uniform development in the increase or decrease in support for the three policy areas, although a reasonable standard of living for the elderly has a mainly negative development in perceptions among citizens. A plausible argument could be that the change in demography in many countries, and the use of words such as 'elderly burden', implies that, despite a possible relative increase in self-interest, as there is a larger number of elderly voters, this has had an impact on citizens' attitudes. Given the overall pressure on welfare spending, if there is higher spending for the old, this could cause a higher level of taxes and duties and/or a reduction

Table 7.3: Development in welfare attitudes from 2008 to 2016 dependent on welfare regime and type of intervention

	Childcare services for working parents, government's responsibility			Standard of living for the unemployed, government's responsibility			Standard of living for the old, government's responsibility		
	2008	2016	Difference	2008	2016	Difference	2008	2016	Difference
Conservative welfare regime									
Belgium	7.28	7.57	0.29***	6.06	6.31	0.25***	7.87	7.81	-0.06
Switzerland	6.47	6.58	0.12	6.28	6.15	-0.13	7.23	7.04	-0.19**
Germany	8.02	8.54	0.52***	6.46	6.04	-0.41***	7.60	7.61	0.01
France	7.14	7.39	0.25	6.12	6.20	0.08	7.94	7.85	-0.09
Netherlands	6.29	6.18	-0.10***	6.31	6.40	0.09	7.72	7.42	-0.30***
Liberal welfare regime									
UK	6.93	6.92	0.00	6.00	5.89	-0.11	8.53	7.84	-0.69***
Ireland	6.82	7.05	0.2***3	6.77	6.57	-0.21***	8.48	7.95	-0.53***
Nordic welfare regime									
Sweden	7.92	7.80	-0.12	7.39	6.96	-0.42***	8.48	8.07	-0.41***
Norway	7.97	8.19	0.22***	7.34	7.35	0.01	8.66	8.23	-0.43***
Finland	8.16	8.00	-0.17***	7.47	7.19	-0.27***	8.44	8.13	-0.31***
South European welfare regime									
Spain	8.36	7.97	-0.38***	8.87	7.84	-1.03***	8.54	7.75	-0.79***
Post-communist welfare regime									
Estonia	8.23	8.40	0.18**	7.26	6.59	-0.67***	8.71	8.40	-0.31***
Czech Republic	7.42	7.95	0.53***	6.30	6.59	0.29***	8.22	8.21	-0.01
Poland	7.27	8.14	0.87***	6.36	6.05	-0.31***	8.65	8.16	-0.49***
Slovenia	8.15	8.31	0.16*	6.75	6.88	0.13	8.34	8.19	-0.16*
Russian Federation	8.15	7.49	-0.66***	7.08	6.45	-0.63***	9.22	8.59	-0.63***
Hungary	8.38	7.72	-0.66***	8.78	6.93	-1.85***	7.78	6.15	-1.63***

Note: Only countries involved in both rounds have been included. Significance level at * 0.05; ** 0.01; *** 0.001.

Source: Calculated using ESS data for 2008 and 2016

in spending in other welfare areas. It could also reflect the debates on pension reforms that have taken place in many European countries.

In order to test how different individual and institutional variables influence welfare attitudes within the three areas, a multi-level regression analysis was conducted. Multi-level regression is used when dealing with hierarchical data. In this study, individuals are nested in countries. In the literature, several competing explanations of welfare attitudes are found (for a discussion of these different theoretical explanations and concepts, see Chapter 2). Here, it is only included for illustrative purposes (see Table 7.4), including variables chosen to represent these possible explanations for the variation in, and reasons for, the development in support. To a large extent, the table is based upon the concept presented in Chapter 2, but also relies on rational understandings as the mechanism includes the traditional economic understanding of the behaviour of individuals. However, the book does not go further into detail in relation to the mechanism. The chosen variables follow a classical aspect, such as socio-economic position, political position and the impact of welfare regimes.

The multi-level regression shows an increase from 2008 to 2016 in support for governmental intervention when it comes to childcare services for working parents, while the support for governmental responsibility for the old and unemployed decreases. It seems that people have adopted 'the social investment paradigm' (see Morel et al, 2012; Midgley et al, 2017), where governmental intervention should mainly be targeted at the productive workforce. At the same time,

Table 7.4: Theoretical explanations related to legitimacy and variables used to measure this

	Theory	Mechanism	Variable
Self-interest	Economic theory	Economic man Calculation of cost/benefit	Income Education Labour market position Age
Ideology	Opinion formation theory	Welfare attitudes based on interests, political values and beliefs	Left–Right scale
Trust	Social theory	Values and attitudes based on trust and solidarity	Interpersonal trust Institutional trust
Welfare institutions	Institutional theory	Welfare attitudes formed by institutions	Welfare regime

this is in contrast with the deserving approach, which has also been one of the criticisms of the social investment approach (Nolan, 2013).

In line with the self-interest hypothesis, the regression also shows that people with higher income are less in favour of governmental responsibilities for childcare services and a reasonable standard of living for the unemployed and the old. People who perceive that they are at risk of poverty are also more likely to support governmental intervention, especially when it comes to supporting governmental responsibility for ensuring a reasonable standard of living for the unemployed.

From this vantage point, people with a lower structural position are in favour of governmental intervention because they are more likely to benefit from the intervention, that is, the self-interest position. Women are also more likely to be in favour of governmental intervention than men, especially when it comes to childcare for working parents. This result is also in line with interest explanations because women often have the main responsibility for unpaid care work in many countries (Lewis, 2001; Steiber and Haas, 2009; Boje and Ejrnæs, 2012). Women, then, have more interest in governmental investment in childcare because it could help them to enter or stay in the labour market, as well as possibly have a better combination of work and family life.

Table 7.5 further shows the average level of government responsibilities among different socio-economic groups when the other relevant variables in the regression are controlled for. The table shows that the unemployed are more in favour of governmental intervention when it comes to ensuring a reasonable standard of living for the unemployed.

Surprisingly, the retired are not more in favour of governmental responsibility in ensuring a reasonable standard of living for the old. This last fact contradicts the self-interest hypothesis because the retired could benefit from more governmental intervention in this area. Part of the explanation might be the difference in long-term care (LTC) and health care as, for example, the state has only limited responsibilities for LTC in Eastern and Southern Europe (Greve, 2017). With less government responsibility and more of a role for the family, the results can be seen as the natural impact of a low level of provision, making it more difficult to see a role for the government.

When it comes to childcare services for working parents, the people in paid work have significantly lower support for governmental responsibility than the reference category. The 'other' category consists of people who are not in work because they are looking after children

Table 7.5: Explaining welfare attitudes – what is important in relation to different welfare areas?

	Childcare services for working parents	Standard of living: unemployment	Standard of living: old
Intercept	8.607***	6.445***	8.535***
2008	–0.138***	0.191***	0.301***
ref: 2016	0	0	0
Income decile 1–10	–0.017***	–0.047***	–0.027***
Years of completed education	–0.013***	–0.010***	–0.021***
Labour market position			
Paid work	–0.087**	–0.167***	–0.052
Education	–0.339***	0.035	–0.054
Unemployment	–0.104*	0.404***	–0.084
Retired	0.123**	–0.108*	0.010
Ref: other	0	0.000	0
Perceived risk of poverty	0.167***	0.304***	0.226***
Ref: no perceived risk of poverty			
Male	–0.218***	–0.063***	–0.084***
Ref: female	0	0.000	0
Children living in home	0.220***	–0.059**	0.031
Ref: no children	0	0.000	0
Age	0.013***	0.022***	0.023***
Age squared	0.000***	–0.0002***	0.000***
Placement Left–Right scale	–0.095***	–0.131***	–0.056***
Institutional trust	0.022***	0.068***	–0.032***
General trust	0.001	0.041***	–0.011*
Continental	–0.753*	–0.374**	–0.666***
Scandinavian	0.161	0.700***	0.184
South Europe	0.192	0.993***	0.298
Anglo-Saxon	–0.988*	–0.371*	–0.105
ref: post-communist			0
n individual	47,143	47,244	47,363
n country	17	17	17
Individual variance	3.813***	4.140***	2.789***
Country-level variance	0.239***	0.030***	0.052***
R square individual	2.5%	4.3%	3.2%
R square country	39.5%	88.2%	70.9%

Notes: Significance level at *0.05; **0.01; ***0.001. The variable of institutional trust is based on five items indicating trust in different institutions. The question about trust was phrased as follows: 'Please tell me on a scale of 0 to 10 how much you personally trust each of the institutions. 0 means you do not trust an institution at all, and 10 means you have complete trust. The institutions are: (1) national parliament; (2) politicians; (3) political parties; (4) the legal system; and (5) the police'. The Cronbach's alpha reliability coefficient for the data was .88. This indicates a very satisfactory correlation between the five items and a high level of internal reliability. The scale goes from 0 (minimum trust) to 10 (maximum) trust as it is intended to capture institutional trust. The variable of perceived risk of poverty is based on following question: 'During the next 12 months, how likely is it that there will be some periods when you don't have enough money to cover your household necessities?'. The variable is recoded into a dummy variable where the answers of 'likely' and 'very likely' indicate perceived risk of poverty while 'not likely' and 'not very likely' are the reference category.

or they are sick. A possible explanation for the higher level of support for childcare services in this category could therefore be that some of them are hindered in getting paid work because of a lack of childcare services.

Inhabitants of the Southern and Nordic welfare states seem to be in favour of, and positive about, state involvement to a larger degree than in the other welfare regimes – and especially when it comes to day care for children. This result is surprising for the Nordic welfare states in the sense that there has been a development towards more care for children in these countries, while, at the same time, this reflects the fact that ideas also influence voters' perceptions of the role of the state (see Chapter 2; see also, eg, Béland, 2005, 2018). Therefore, there is a dual possible impact of, and interaction between, voters and decision-makers in relation to attitudes towards welfare state development. The causal direction between ideas, perceptions and development might thus be difficult to disentangle as the existing context, as argued earlier for LTC, also has an impact on attitudes.

The regression analysis also shows that ideology in terms of placement on a Left–Right scale has a significant influence on support for governmental responsibility. People with right-wing sympathies are less likely to think that it is the government's responsibility to ensure childcare and a reasonable standard of living for the unemployed and the old. However, the relationship between support for governmental intervention and ideological belief differs between the three policy areas. The size of the coefficient on the regression analysis indicates that the correlation between ideology and governmental responsibility for unemployment is much stronger than in the other two areas. This means that when it comes to ensuring a decent life for the unemployed, governmental responsibility is more influenced by the respondent's ideological stance on a traditional Left–Right scale than the other two areas. One explanation could be that ensuring a reasonable standard of living for the unemployed involves more class-based redistribution, which traditionally follows the Left–Right scale, while a reasonable standard of living for the old and childcare for working parents is more a redistribution across generations. This is also in line with the argument that in some welfare states, the middle class has been 'bribed' to support the welfare state, and this fits well with the use of childcare. To put it another way, public expenditure mainly benefits higher social groups, as pointed out already a long time ago (LeGrand, 1982). This is sometimes also labelled the Matthew effect and can be witnessed not only in the field of childcare, but also in social investment policies, including active labour market policy

(Bonoli and Liechti, 2018). Furthermore, the unemployed are often seen as less deserving (on the viewpoints of people on unemployment benefit, see also the quotes in Chapter 6).

In the literature, it is often claimed that a condition for welfare redistribution is that people trust their fellow citizens, as well as political and legal institutions (see Chapter 2; see also Svallfors, 2013). The social contract that is the foundation of welfare redistribution depends on people trusting each other, as well as political and legal institutions. The regression analysis shows a rather interesting result when it comes to the effect of institutional trust on governmental responsibilities. People with a high level of institutional trust are more in favour of governmental responsibilities when it comes to ensuring a reasonable standard of living for the unemployed and childcare. However, given the in-depth stories presented in Chapter 6, the reason could be that if there is trust in government, then one is less expectant of low levels of efficiency and justice in the delivery of services. Surprisingly, people with high institutional trust are less in favour of governmental responsibilities in ensuring a reasonable standard of living for the old (see Figure 7.1); however, as argued, existing levels of services can influence viewpoints. A possible explanation could therefore be that people with low institutional trust also think that the government

Figure 7.1: Institutional trust and attitudes to different welfare areas, 2008–16

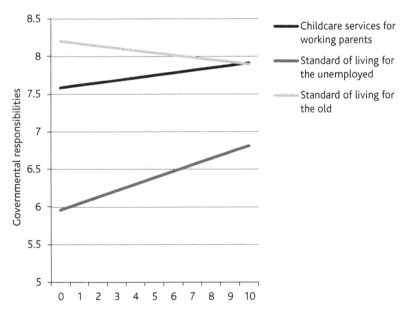

Source: Own calculation based on the regression analysis of ESS 2008 and 2016 data

should, in fact, provide a higher pension and better services for the old. There might also be an issue with the fact that there is a connection between income and institutional trust, so that some with a high income have low institutional trust and are less likely to use benefit systems, and thus less likely to have a self-interest in supporting LTC or do not expect to be eligible to receive the benefit.

One explanation could be that if there is institutional trust, then the fear of misuse of the system will be less strong. While this does not explain the falling slope in relation to the standard of living for the old, this might reflect an overall more positive stance, and a higher proportion of those having less institutional trust, either themselves or in general, find that older people are more deserving. However, at the same time, it is not always clear that the perception of misuse actually reflects the size of misuse of the system.

When it comes to interpersonal trust (see Figure 7.2), on the one hand, there is a positive correlation between interpersonal trust and attitudes in favour of governmental responsibility for ensuring a reasonable standard of living for the unemployed. On the other hand, there is a negative correlation between interpersonal trust and support for governmental responsibility for ensuring a reasonable standard of living for the old.

Figure 7.2: Interpersonal trust and attitudes to different welfare areas, 2008–16

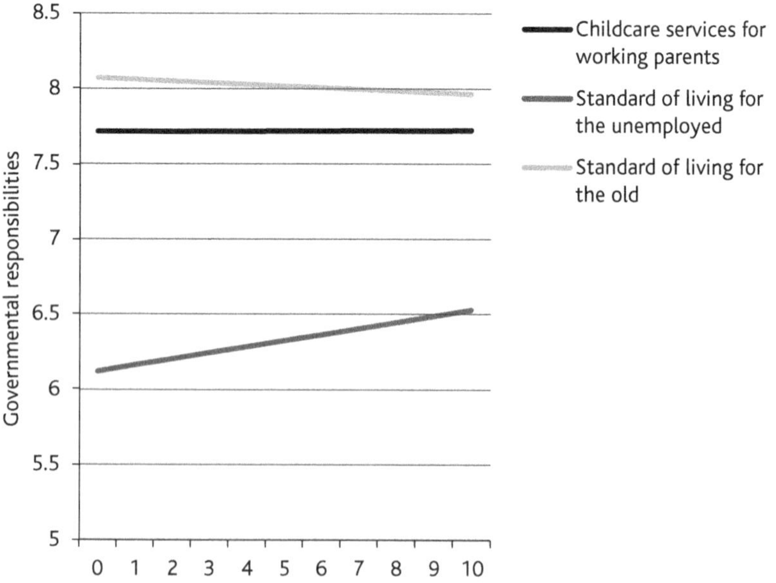

Source: Based upon ESS data

Following Arts and Gelissen (2001: 285), we can distinguish between two forms of solidarity: 'Solidarity takes shape either vertically: The "strong" help the "weak" by redistributing benefits and burdens, or horizontally: The "strong" and the "weak" contribute to the common weal by risk-sharing'. It seems that supporting governmental intervention when it comes to unemployment is much more dependent on vertical solidarity between the better off compared to the less well off, where the stronger 'permanently employed' help the weak 'unemployed' rather than supporting governmental intervention when it comes to the old. As interpersonal trust links people who are different from ourselves, it also reflects concern for vulnerable groups such as the unemployed, and could contribute to vertical solidarity (Rothstein and Uslaner, 2005). One of the reasons why interpersonal trust has a weak negative effect on governmental responsibility for the old could be that the general assumption is that the old deserve benefits from the state.

The last theoretical explanation is that welfare state institutions influence support for governmental intervention, for example, for childcare (see Chung and Meuleman, 2017). According to this perspective, the Nordic welfare states, with their more generous universalistic welfare system (see Greve, 2018), will be more likely to support governmental responsibility when it comes to supporting the unemployed, the old and families with children. The regression shows, as expected, that people in the Nordic countries are more likely to support the fact that governments have a responsibility to support childcare services, the unemployed and the old. When it comes to support for the unemployed, in particular, people from the Nordic countries are much more likely to think that it is the government's responsibility to ensure a reasonable standard of living. Support for governmental responsibility is also relatively high among people in Southern European countries and post-communist countries (see Table 7.6).

In the liberal welfare states, we find the lowest level of support for governmental responsibility when it comes to ensuring childcare for working parents. An explanation could be the tradition of means-tested benefits in the liberal welfare states, and the late development of welfare services (see also Chapter 5), implying that only few people benefit from it; thus, the causal relation might also be difficult to depict. The Continental countries are less likely to want governmental responsibility for supporting a reasonable standard of living for the old. One explanation could be that the Continental European pension system is, to a higher degree, built on mandatory insurance.

Table 7.6: Welfare regime and average attitudes to different welfare areas

	Childcare services for working parents	Standard of living for the unemployed	Standard of living for the old
Continental countries	7.2	6.3	7.6
Scandinavian countries	8.1	7.4	8.5
Southern European countries	8.1	7.7	8.6
Anglo-Saxon countries	6.9	6.3	8.2
Post-communist countries	7.9	6.7	8.3

Source: Own calculations based on the regression analysis of ESS data for 2016 and 2008

Furthermore, as in Southern and Eastern Europe, there is a larger role for families in the delivery of LTC, the implication again being that a limited public service might in itself reduce support as there are presumably some who already have to pay for services themselves. Thus, support for welfare services might be stronger if there are also services available for the middle class.

The fact that there might be a curvilinear relation between age and welfare attitudes is confirmed in Figure 7.3. However, the age at which maximum support for governmental responsibility can be found varies between the three policy areas. The figure shows that people are most

Figure 7.3: Age and attitudes to different welfare areas

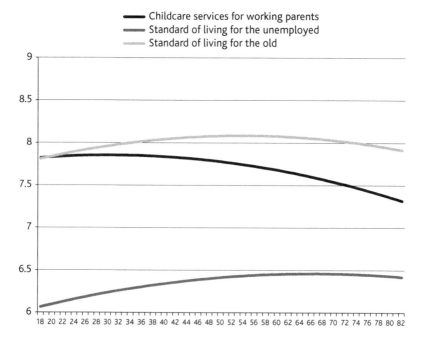

supportive of governmental responsibility for childcare at the age of 30, while it is 66 and 53 years for governmental responsibility for the unemployed and the old, respectively. Again, it is surprising that the highest level of support for governmental responsibility for the old is before the age of retirement, although this might reflect the fact that people at this time of their life are starting to be aware of the standard of living for the old, and that some of those who have reached that age are feeling well. Support for childcare at the age of 30 fits well with the fact that many people have their first child around this age, and this is also in line with the self-interest argument.

Figure 7.3 depicts that the elderly, with the exception of childcare services, are more positive and in favour of welfare state support overall. Part of this might reflect self-interest, but also historical knowledge on the possible negative impact of a high level of unemployment on the standard of living. A rather surprising result is that the different individual variables show relatively small amounts of variance in welfare attitudes. This points to more stable support for the welfare state, although this might be influenced by external shocks and changes in ideas.

Other data

Eurobarometer surveys have monitored, for example, attitudes related to migration, pensions and so on, including satisfaction with life and various other issues. Appendix 7.1 shows the development in overall satisfaction with life within the EU. Overall, despite going up and down, it is overwhelmingly positive. There was a downturn after the financial crisis, as one would expect, but since 2014, it has been higher than before the financial crisis. Therefore, in this way, one should not expect a more critical stance towards welfare spending and migrants at the outset given that satisfaction with life in general is good. The number not satisfied is also still at a very low level. The impact of the financial crisis can also be witnessed in Figure 7.4.

Trust in national government declined substantially in the wake of the crisis, and has still not got back to previous levels. The image of the EU also declined in the wake of the financial crisis, so that in 2012, 30% had a positive image of the EU, compared to 50% in 2006, although rising again to 40% in 2018 (European Commission, 2018). Naturally, there is national variation, but this is an indication that the economic crisis influenced voters' perception of whether they can trust the EU, with migration and free movement within the EU perhaps being one reason. Thus, a change in perception and support

Figure 7.4: Trust in the national government (OECD 33) from 2005/06 to 2014–16

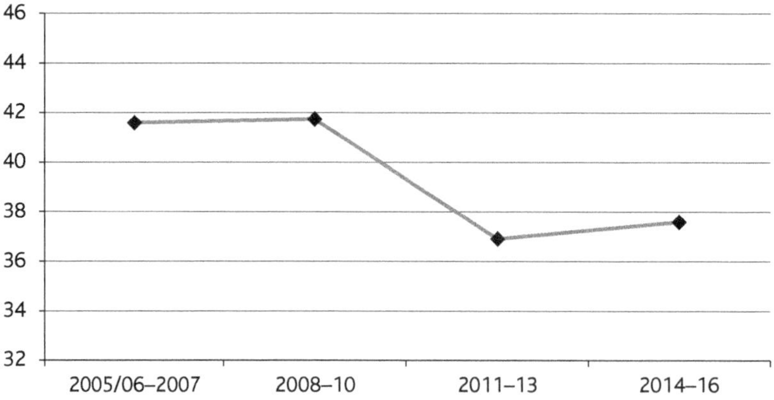

Source: OECD (2017: Figure 1.29)

for institutions can be influenced by external economic shocks, which also helps in understanding populist support.

This is also the case, albeit not to the same degree, when looking at trust in politicians. Using the ESS, since it was enacted, there has gradually been a decline in trust, especially from 2002 to 2004 and again from 2014 to 2016 (see Table 7.7), albeit that the change is not very strong over time.

Lack of trust in politicians opens the way for populism to be used in order to gain votes more easily as this can reflect a 'them and us' approach, or that the bureaucrats/elite who are the existing politicians cannot be trusted. In this way, this reflects the seemingly growing tendency towards welfare chauvinism (see more in Chapter 8).

In Table 7.8 is shown the development in trust in governments in selected EU countries since 2004 (if the survey took place in both the spring and autumn, then the autumn measurement is used).

The table confirms, albeit with variation, that the economic crisis had an impact on trust, but it also shows a difference between the Nordic welfare states, with a higher tendency to trust government in general, and the Southern European welfare states, where it is low.

Table 7.7: Trust in politicians since 2002

ESS round	2002	2004	2006	2008	2010	2012	2014	2016
Trust in politicians	4.05	3.86	3.90	3.96	3.79	3.92	3.88	4.03

Source: Calculation based on answers to the ESS question on trust in politicians, ranging from not at all (given value 0) to complete trust (given value 10) for the 12 countries who participated in both surveys

Table 7.8: Trust in government since 2004 in selected countries

	2004	2008	2012	2016	2018
EU	33.6	34	27.2	31.3	33.7
Denmark	56	60.3	42.2	42.8	46.7
Czech Republic	27.2	20	10.7	28.2	27.5
France	29.5	30.9	29.9	16.8	31.3
Germany	33.1	42.4	40.7	50.8	54.3
Ireland	38.6	32.7	18.4	39.7	45.6
Italy	28.4	25.8	16.4	14.9	15.4
Poland	12.8	19.5	23.4	25.7	28.1
Spain	51.1	44.1	11.3	19.5	16.8
Sweden	41.3	56.2	58.7	56.3	59.6
UK	32.1	29.3	24.9	35.2	31.1

Source: 'Public opinion in EU'. Available at: http://ec.europa.eu/commfrontoffice/publicopinion/index.cfm (accessed 30 August 2018)

Changes might naturally reflect specific national circumstances. Still, a crisis is not good for trust – or for the happiness of the people.

Conclusion

There has been a decline in trust in the central government, although less so in politicians, which might help in explaining the development towards a more populist and nativist stance with regard to social policy in several countries around Europe. At the same time, there has not been any strong negative reduction in the support for the welfare state, seemingly indicating that right- as well as left-wing populist parties presumably support welfare states to a higher extent than one could have expected at the outset.

At the same time, this is in line with the fact that although there has been retrenchment in certain parts of the welfare state (for details, see Chapter 5), this is not the overall picture, and support for care and income to those seen by the people as seemingly deserving has an impact on the political system's decisions. In this way, it is not only ideas at the decision level that have an impact on welfare state development, but also the other way around. An interesting issue is how, on the one hand, support for part of the welfare state can be found, while, on the other hand, there is increasing inequality (as depicted in Chapter 3), as well as increasingly a risk of a more dualised labour market (which is shown in Chapter 4).

Those with higher levels of trust are also more supportive of the development of the welfare state. The existing level of provision also seems to influence support, and support for social policy is higher in the more universalistic welfare states than in countries normally depicted as belonging to other welfare regimes.

Welfare chauvinism cannot be directly shown by the data (see more in Chapter 8), but the attitudes and change thereof indicate that welfare chauvinism has come more to the fore of the agenda than it was earlier. This helps explain why different parts of the welfare state are under attack compared to others, with the highest support across welfare regimes for a reasonable standard of living for the old, then children and, last, for the unemployed.

Note

[1] On welfare attitudes in Europe, see the regional issue of *Social Policy & Administration* (2018), 52(4).

References

Arts, W. and Gelissen, J. (2001) Welfare states, solidarity and justice principles: does the type really matter? *Acta Sociologica*, 44(4): 283–99.

Béland, D. (2005) Ideas and social policy: an institutionalist perspective. *Social Policy & Administration*, 39(1): 1–18.

Béland, D. (2018) How ideas impact social policy. In B. Greve (ed) *The Routledge handbook of the welfare state* (2nd edn). Oxon: Routledge.

Boje, T.P. and Ejrnæs, A. (2012) Policy and practice: the relationship between family policy regime and women's labour market participation in Europe. *International Journal of Sociology and Social Policy*, 32(9/10): 589–605.

Bonoli, G. and Liechti, F. (2018) Good intentions and Matthe effects: access biases in participation in active labour market policies. *Journal of European Public Policy*, 25(6): 894–911.

Chung, H. and Meuleman, B. (2017) European parents' attitudes towards public childcare provision: the role of current provisions, interests and ideologies. *European Societies*, 19(1): 49–68.

Chung, H., Taylor-Gooby, P. and Leruth, B. (2018) Introduction. *Social Policy & Administration*, 52(4): 835–46.

Dahlberg, M., Edmark, K. and Lundqvist, H. (2012) Ethnic diversity and preferences for redistribution. *Journal of Political Economy*, 120(1): 41–76.

Ervasti, H. and Hjerm, M. (2012) Immigration, trust and support for the welfare state. In H. Ervasti, J.G. Andersen; T. Fridberg, and K. Ringdahl (eds) *The future of the welfare state: Social policy attitudes and social capital in Europe*. Cheltenham: Edward Elgar.

European Commission (2018) *Public opinion in the European Union*. Standard Eurobarometer 89, Spring, Brussels: European Commission.

European Social Survey (2012) Welfare attitudes in Europe. Topline results from round 4 of the European Social Survey. ESS Topline Results Series, Issue 2.

Greve, B. (ed) (2017) *Long-term care for the elderly in Europe: Development and prospects*. Oxon: Routledge.

Greve, B. (ed) (2018) *The Routledge handbook of the welfare state* (2nd edn). Oxon: Routledge.

LeGrand, J. (1982) *The strategy of equality: Redistribution and the social services*. London: Allen & Unwin.

Lewis, J. (2001) The decline of the male breadwinner model: implications for work and care. *Social Politics: International Studies in Gender, State & Society*, 8(2): 152–69.

Midgley, J., Dahl, E. and Wright, A. (eds) (2017) *Social investment and social welfare: International and critical perspectives*. Cheltenham: Edward Elgar.

Morel, N., Palier, B. and Palme J. (eds) (2012) *Towards a social investment welfare state? Ideas, policies and challenges*. Bristol: Policy Press.

Nolan, B. (2013) What use is 'social investment'? *Journal of European Social Policy*, 23(5): 459–68.

OECD (2017) *How's life? 2017 measuring well-being*. Paris: OECD.

Rothstein, B. and Uslaner, E.M. (2005) All for all: equality, corruption, and social trust. *World Politics*, 58(1): 41–72.

Steiber, N. and Haas, B. (2009) Ideals or compromises? The attitude–behaviour relationship in mothers' employment. *Socio-Economic Review*, 7(4): 639–68.

Stockemer, D. (2017) The success of radical right-wing parties in Western European regions – new challenging findings. *Journal of Contemporary European Studies*, 25(1): 41–56.

Svallfors, S. (2013) Government quality, egalitarianism, and attitudes to taxes and social spending: a European comparison. *European Political Science Review*, 5(3): 363–80.

Svallfors, S. (2014) Welfare attitudes in context. In S. Svallfors (ed) *Welfare attitudes and beyond*. Stanford, CA: Stanford University Press.

Appendix 7.1: Satisfaction with life within the EU since 1993

Date	Very satisfied (%)	Fairly satisfied (%)	Not very satisfied (%)	Not at all satisfied (%)	Don't know (%)
01/09/1973	21.0	58.0	16.0	4.0	1.0
01/05/1975	18.9	57.0	16.0	5.2	2.8
11/10/1975	19.1	55.6	17.6	5.8	1.9
07/05/1976	20.2	54.3	18.5	6.0	1.1
02/11/1976	20.2	56.1	17.0	5.8	0.8
19/04/1977	20.2	54.6	18.2	6.0	1.0
24/10/1977	22.0	56.5	15.6	5.3	0.7
05/05/1978	22.0	55.1	16.3	5.9	0.8
15/11/1978	21.6	56.5	15.7	5.4	0.8
05/04/1979	20.5	57.0	16.2	5.1	1.1
08/04/1980	21.2	57.6	15.4	4.9	0.8
23/03/1981	21.3	54.2	16.9	6.1	1.6
22/03/1982	23.7	56.7	14.2	4.1	1.2
02/10/1982	21.3	56.4	16.2	5.1	1.0
25/03/1983	20.0	57.7	15.6	6.0	0.8
27/09/1983	18.3	58.2	16.0	5.9	1.7
14/03/1984	21.8	55.5	15.9	5.6	1.3
02/10/1984	19.7	59.3	16.0	4.0	1.0
14/03/1985	22.9	56.6	15.2	4.6	0.7
15/10/1985	17.8	56.7	18.4	5.9	1.1
19/03/1986	22.5	57.5	14.7	4.6	0.8
30/09/1986	19.3	57.0	17.1	5.3	1.2
17/03/1987	22.6	56.8	15.4	4.4	0.9
05/10/1987	20.5	55.0	16.9	6.7	0.9
18/03/1988	23.6	57.7	13.9	4.0	0.8
17/10/1988	19.9	48.6	26.0	4.8	0.7
13/03/1989	23.5	59.4	12.7	3.7	0.7
03/10/1989	22.3	59.4	13.7	3.8	0.6
19/03/1990	25.8	56.8	12.5	4.3	0.5
10/10/1990	19.9	60.7	13.8	4.7	0.6
04/03/1991	23.9	58.7	13.3	3.6	0.4
15/10/1991	23.0	57.9	14.1	4.2	0.7
18/03/1992	22.0	57.7	15.2	4.5	0.5
21/09/1992	22.0	57.6	15.0	4.7	0.6
13/03/1993	21.8	58.0	15.0	4.8	0.4
18/10/1993	19.8	58.7	16.6	4.5	0.3
04/04/1994	20.1	58.9	16.2	4.3	0.5

(continued)

Date	Very satisfied (%)	Fairly satisfied (%)	Not very satisfied (%)	Not at all satisfied (%)	Don't know (%)
28/11/1994	19.9	60.7	14.5	4.4	0.5
27/02/1996	25.9	56.6	13.7	3.1	0.6
26/03/1997	18.9	58.4	17.2	4.7	0.9
07/04/1998	18.7	58.6	17.1	4.6	0.9
15/10/1999	19.6	61.9	14.2	3.3	1.0
05/04/2000	16.6	60.3	18.3	4.0	0.8
14/11/2000	20.7	62.2	13.2	3.1	0.7
12/04/2001	21.1	61.6	13.6	2.8	0.9
13/10/2001	21.4	61.6	13.2	3.0	0.8
29/03/2002	20.8	61.8	13.7	2.9	0.8
01/10/2002	18.7	61.7	15.1	3.7	0.9
01/10/2003	19.4	59.5	16.5	3.5	1.2
02/10/2004	22.7	58.3	14.6	4.0	0.4
09/05/2005	20.8	59.7	15.3	3.7	0.6
27/03/2006	20.6	61.0	14.5	3.7	0.3
06/09/2006	21.9	60.4	13.7	3.6	0.4
10/04/2007	20.7	60.2	14.6	4.0	0.4
22/09/2007	20.5	59.7	15.5	3.9	0.4
25/03/2008	18.8	58.4	17.2	5.1	0.5
01/10/2008	18.2	58.4	17.9	5.0	0.5
01/06/2009	21.2	56.1	17.0	5.2	0.5
05/05/2010	20.7	56.6	16.4	5.9	0.4
11/11/2010	20.4	57.5	16.2	5.5	0.4
06/05/2011	21.3	57.6	15.4	5.1	0.6
05/11/2011	19.3	55.9	18.5	5.6	0.6
12/05/2012	20.8	55.5	16.8	6.4	0.5
03/11/2012	19.9	55.7	17.4	6.5	0.4
10/05/2013	20.5	54.7	17.8	6.6	0.4
02/11/2013	20.2	55.3	17.6	6.6	0.3
31/05/2014	23.9	56.3	14.7	4.8	0.3
08/11/2014	23.4	56.0	15.7	4.5	0.3
16/05/2015	22.9	57.1	15.3	4.3	0.3
07/11/2015	24.1	57.2	14.6	3.9	0.3
21/05/2016	24.6	55.4	15.1	4.5	0.3
03/11/2016	23.9	57.5	14.3	4.0	0.4
20/05/2017	25.4	56.8	13.4	4.0	0.3
11/2017	24.6	57.9	13.5	3.6	0.5
03/2018	23.4	59.5	13.4	3.2	0.5

Source: Eurobarometer (accessed 27 September 2017 and 24 October 2018)

Populism, welfare chauvinism and hostility towards immigrants

Anders Ejrnæs and Bent Greve

Introduction

This chapter looks into the development in populism, welfare chauvinism and hostility towards immigrants in different welfare regimes. As depicted both in the theoretical chapters and in Chapter 7, it seems that attitudes towards those who, rightly or wrongly, are taking jobs and/or using the benefit system can help in the deeper understanding of populism and welfare chauvinism. Immigration has been the most important issue among citizens since 2014, except in early 2017, when terrorism was higher. Close to 40% overall, and in the second half of 2015, close to 60%, of survey respondents found that this was the most important issue. Before that, the financial crisis and economic development were more important (European Commission, 2018). Thus, there is a good reason to look into whether immigration also has an impact that can be related to populism.

In order to analyse the link between rising populism, anti-immigrant sentiments, welfare chauvinism and economic insecurity in Europe, we compare the development in six European countries (Germany, the UK, France, Hungary, Spain and Sweden), representing different welfare regimes. The chapter will analyse whether the rise in populism reflects growing welfare chauvinism and hostility towards immigrants and refugees. As the selected countries represent different welfare regimes and political systems, we will analyse varieties of welfare chauvinism and attitudes towards immigrants and a multicultural society. In the last part of the chapter, we will analyse to what extent perceived economic insecurity shapes opinions towards an outgroup such as immigrants, and whether we see a growing polarisation in attitude between the economically secure and the economically vulnerable and insecure. The chapter proceed by looking into the rise in populism, understood as support for populist parties, followed by looking into attitudes towards immigrants and refugees, and, finally, by looking at whether one can find traits towards welfare chauvinist opinions.

Rise in populism

Over previous decades, we have seen rising support for populist parties in many Western countries (see also Chapters 1 and 2). The mean voter share of populist Right parties has been increasing in most European countries. Figure 8.1 shows that in Sweden, Germany, Hungary and the UK, the vote share has increased over previous decades. In the most recent election in 2017 in Germany, the support for the Alternative Für Deutschland (AFD) Party has increased to 12.6%. In Sweden, in the election in September 2018, the immigrant-critical party got 17.6%[1] of the votes. A central question is whether the rise in support for populist parties reflects growing anti-immigrant sentiment, an opposition to multiculturalism and growing welfare chauvinism.

There are several possible explanations for the growing support for populist parties. Some of the most prominent theories on the demand side are the economic inequality/insecurity perspective, on the one hand, and the cultural backlash theory, on the other (Inglehart and Norris, 2016). The first perspective focuses on how growing inequality in the post-industrial economy divides people into winners and losers

Figure 8.1: Vote share of right-wing populist parties (national election)

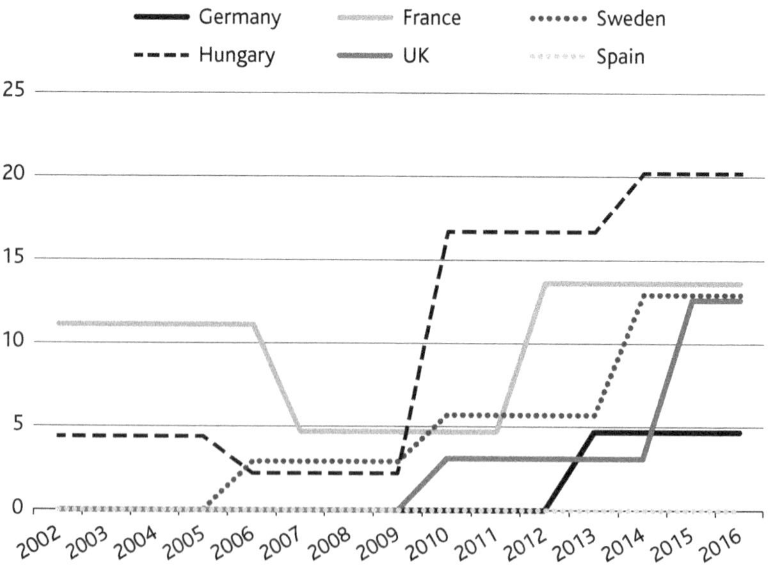

Source: Comparative Political Data Set (CPDS)

of the global economy (see also Chapter 4). As a consequence of growing inequality, the insecure segment will blame outgroups, such as immigrants, for their own lack of opportunities and inadequate welfare services. The 'cultural backlash thesis' explains growing support for populist parties as a counter-reaction to the broader shift towards more post-materialist values in society, such as multiculturalism and cosmopolitanism. In line with cultural backlash theory, growing support for populist parties is seen as a consequence of the rising numbers of immigrants and asylum seekers, and hostility towards immigrants and a multicultural society. In the next sections, we will analyse some of the developments in attitudes towards immigrants and their right to social benefits.

Attitudes towards immigrants and refugees

In theory, one could argue that if there is a negative attitude towards immigrants and refugees, then this could fuel a more welfare chauvinist approach as they will be seen as outsiders and as not having the same right to benefits as the native population (see also Chapter 2). This might reflect a position among citizens that migrants get more from the state than they contribute. In Table 8.1, the possible position is described.

In Table 8.1 the lower the value, the more it is the perception that migrants get more than they contribute. Therefore, this shows that the feeling is especially strong in the Czech Republic, Austria and Hungary, all with values below 4. The highest value in 2014 was in Sweden, indicating that, at least at that time, migrants were not in general seen as relying on the welfare state. Another interesting issue is that, with the exception of Austria, Portugal and Spain, the development from 2002 shows that there seems to be less fear that migrants take out more than they contribute.

A central question is to what extent the rise of populist parties reflects a growing hostility towards immigration and a multicultural society. This is investigated by Figure 8.2, which looks into the position related to how generous the government should be in judging applications for refugee status.

Figure 8.2 shows that the share of the population that opposes the generous judging of applications for refugee status is increasing in all countries except the UK, being more or less the same in Spain, Norway, Ireland and Switzerland from 2014 to 2016. It further shows strong variation across European Union (EU) countries, and not seemingly following a welfare regime approach. The increased

Table 8.1: Do immigrants gets more than they contribute, 2002–14

	2014	2002
Austria	3.9	4.4
Belgium	4.3	4.0
Switzerland	4.7	4.3
Czech Republic	3.7	3.6
Germany	4.9	3.9
Denmark	4.7	4.2
Spain	4.0	4.7
Finland	4.6	4.2
France	4.4	4.4
UK	4.6	4.0
Hungary	3.9	3.6
Ireland	4.2	3.7
Netherlands	4.4	4.3
Norway	5.0	4.7
Poland	4.7	4.2
Portugal	4.7	5.5
Sweden	5.5	4.7
Slovenia	4.8	4.4
Total	4.5	4.2

Note: The question used in 2002 and 2014 was: 'Most people who come to live here work and pay taxes. They also use health and welfare services. On balance, do you think people who come here take out more than they put in or put in more than they take out?'. Answers range from 'generally take out more' (coded 1) to 'generally take out less' (coded 9). Only countries with data from before and after the financial crisis are included.

Source: European Social Survey (ESS) 2002 and 2014

opposition to refugees is not very surprising considering the increasing number of refugees that several countries have received. This also raises the question as to whether countries should reduce the number of immigrants, especially those coming from outside the EU who countries can control (as it is not possible to control immigrants from within the EU, who can claim status as migrant workers under the freedom of movement). This is depicted in Figure 8.3.

Figure 8.3 surprisingly shows that the share of people having anti-immigration sentiments is not on rise. The share of the population that would allow few or no immigrants is either decreasing or stable in all countries except Hungary, the Czech Republic, Poland and Austria. The two figures illustrate that the change in opinion towards a more restrictive refugee policy does not reflect a more negative stance on immigration. A possible explanation of the more positive, or the less negative, attitudes towards immigrants could be growing labour

Figure 8.2: Government should be generous when judging applications for refugee status – 'disagree' and 'disagree strongly'

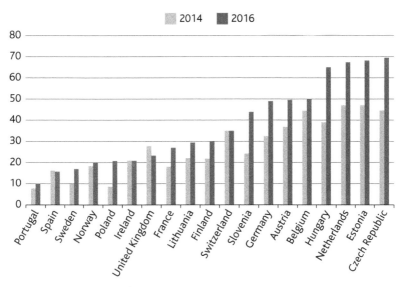

Source: ESS 2014 and 2016 (all European countries that have participated in both rounds are included). The question about judging applications for refugee status is only covered in ESS 2014 and 2016.

Figure 8.3: Allow few/no immigrants from poorer countries outside Europe

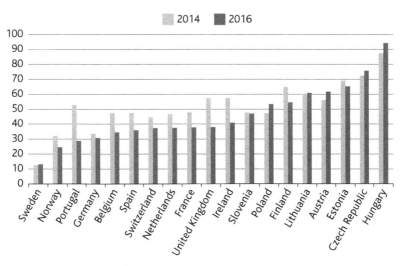

Source: ESS 2014 and 2016 (all European countries that have participated in both rounds are included)

shortages due to economic development in some of the countries. At the same time, even if there are people with a negative stance towards migrants, there are others who, in the light of the crisis, might perceive it in a more positive way, and also countries that have a colonial history.

Hungary and Sweden represent two extremes. In Hungary, 94% of the population would allow no or few immigrants from poorer countries, while only 13% of the Swedish population state that they would allow no or few immigrants from poorer countries. The huge difference between the two countries when it comes to immigration from poorer countries could reflect huge difference in the political discourse in the two countries. Thereby, this also implies that there need not be a connection between the numbers of refugees and those having a negative stance; rather, this could reflect ideological positions and political priorities in individual countries.

A constant discussion has been whether part of the changes can be argued to be related to the movement towards a more multicultural society (see also the narratives in Chapter 6). This is not necessarily easy to measure. In order to measure the development in attitudes towards a multicultural society, we have constructed an index. This has been done by using three items in the European Social Survey (ESS) measuring support for multicultural attitudes. The questions used are the following:

- 'Would you say it is generally bad or good for [country's] economy that people come to live here from other countries? Please use this card.' Measured on a scale from 0 (bad for the economy) to 10 (good for the economy).
- 'And, using this card, would you say that [country's] cultural life is generally undermined or enriched by people coming to live here from other countries?' Measured on a scale from 0 (cultural life undermined) to 10 (cultural life enriched).
- 'Is [country] made a worse or a better place to live by people coming to live here from other countries? Please use this card.' Measured on a scale from 0 (worse place to live) to 10 (better place to live).

In this scale, 10 indicates an extremely positive attitude towards immigrants and a multicultural society, while 0 indicates an extremely negative attitude towards multiculturalism. In Figure 8.4, the development in the degree of a positive attitude is shown for the six countries. Each question has been given the same weight; therefore, the higher average, the more positive the attitude.

Figure 8.4: Positive attitudes towards a multicultural society (0–10)

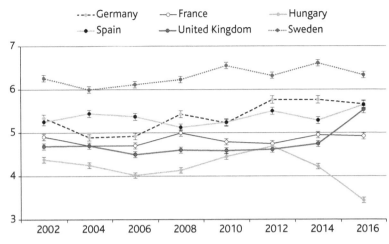

Source: ESS rounds 1 to 8

Figure 8.4 shows that attitudes towards a multicultural society are relative stable over time in Germany, Spain, France and Sweden. Once more, we find no evidence that the rise in populist parties reflects a growing hostility towards immigrants and a multicultural society. In Hungary, in contrast, we see a rapid decline in support for a multicultural society from 2012 to 2016, while in UK, we see a rise in support for a multicultural society. The rapid decline in support for a multicultural society in Hungary could reflect the fact that the political elite has adopted a more nativist stance to a larger extent. The growing support for a multicultural society in the UK could be a reason why some, as a counter-reaction, supported Brexit and voted to leave the EU in the belief that a multicultural society would then be an issue for the UK to decide upon alone.

If we look at the development in attitudes towards a multicultural society in all European countries covered by the ESS, we find that in East and Central Europe and Italy, support for immigration and a multicultural society has declined while support is either stable or on the rise in the other European countries (see Figure 8.5).

Given the rise in support for populist parties, it is surprising that attitudes towards a multicultural society have not, in general, decreased in more countries. Part of this might reflect the fact that the issue has moved higher up the agenda (see earlier in the chapter). As this issue is seen as the most important, and has thus also been a more important topic for voters, so they have moved to parties taking this as a central

Figure 8.5: Positive attitudes towards a multicultural society

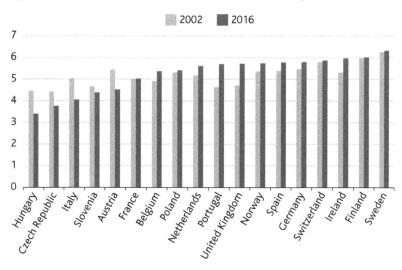

Source: ESS rounds 1 and 8, based on the three items mentioned earlier

issue and having suggestions for how to reduce migration, even if overall perceptions have not changed.

Welfare chauvinism

Welfare chauvinism can be seen as a possible reason for support for populist parties, and also changes in the conditionality of benefits (see more in Chapter 2). In this section, we will analyse whether we see a move in opinion towards more welfare chauvinism, where welfare benefits should be reserved to natives or be more generous to natives than to migrants.

Thus, in this way, the context of the movement towards more populist approaches should seemingly be more influenced by classical issues, at least until 2014, when immigration and terrorism came higher on the agenda (see Chapter 1). In this way, the more classical issue of deserving/undeserving could be assumed to be more important. We try to measure this by looking into when migrants should obtain rights to benefits (see Figure 8.6).

Figure 8.6 shows that despite the large influx of refugees, attitudes towards immigrants' rights to benefits have not changed very much. In both Germany and the UK, attitudes towards immigrants' right to benefits were more generous in 2016 than in 2008, while we see the opposite tendency in Hungary. Despite the relatively small changes in

Figure 8.6: When should immigrants obtain rights to social benefits/services, 2008 and 2016

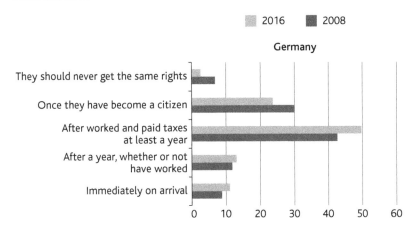

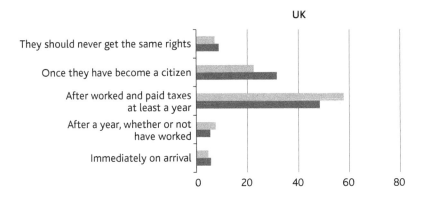

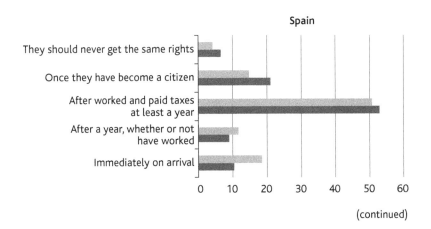

(continued)

Figure 8.6: When should immigrants obtain rights to social benefits/services, 2008 and 2016 (continued)

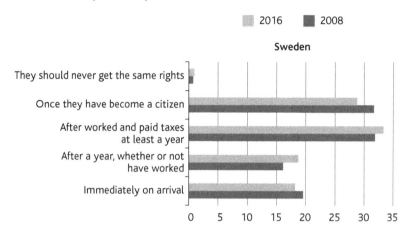

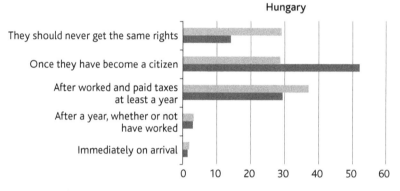

Source: Based upon ESS 2008 and 2016, welfare attitudes question

attitudes across the time period, we find some marked differences in people's attitudes towards immigrants' rights to social benefits across the four countries. In Sweden, approximately 37% think that immigrants should obtain rights to social benefits and services immediately or after one year. In Hungary, approximately 29% think that immigrants should obtain rights to benefits when they become citizens, and 29% think that immigrants should never get the same rights. In Germany, France, Spain and the UK, the majority think that immigrants should obtain rights after they have worked and paid taxes. The variation in the attitudes towards immigrants in the three countries reflects both differences in welfare regimes and differences in citizenship regimes. The attitude in Sweden reflects a welfare system that has a tradition of giving universal access to social benefits and services to all residents.

The high proportion in Spain, France and Germany thinking that immigrants should obtain rights to social benefits when they work and pay taxes could reflect the dualism in welfare benefit and labour market rights.

The more restrictive attitude towards immigrants' social rights in Hungary reflects the fact that welfare chauvinism is on the rise in Hungary, and therefore the attitude that welfare benefits should be restricted to certain groups.

Economic insecurity and polarisation in attitudes towards immigrants

According to the economic insecurity thesis, the rising support for populism reflects a growing division between the winners and losers of globalisation and migration (Lubbers et al, 2002; Standing 2011; Inglehardt and Norris, 2016). The winners make up an economically secure segment benefiting from globalisation and often exhibit a more cosmopolitan lifestyle. The losers make up the economically vulnerable groups that feel threatened by immigrants, who are perceived as outsiders who take their jobs and benefits and challenge their lifestyles (see Chapter 6). In Figure 8.7, we analyse whether subjective economic insecurity (reported difficulties living on current household income) has an impact on attitudes towards immigrants and multiculturalism.

The figures show that in all countries and for all time points, except for Hungary in 2016, people who experience economic insecurity are less in favour of a multicultural society. In Germany, France, Sweden and, to some extent, the UK, the attitude gap is widening between the economically secure and economically insecure. Support for a multicultural society seems to rise among the economically secure and support for immigration and a multicultural society is either stagnating or falling among people living in economic insecurity. The widening attitude gap could indicate a growing polarisation in Western countries, which could threaten social cohesion. Hungary differs from the other countries. The gap between the economically secure and insecure has diminished over time. Contrary to the other countries, the economically secure in Hungary display a rapid decline in support for a multicultural society. This tendency could reflect the fact that the political and bureaucratic elite has a adopted a more nativist stance.

Figure 8.7: Economic insecurity and attitudes towards a multicultural society – different countries

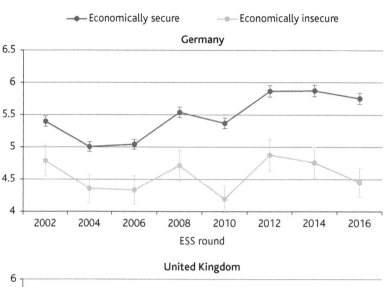

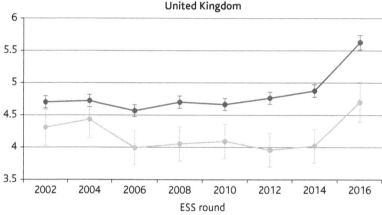

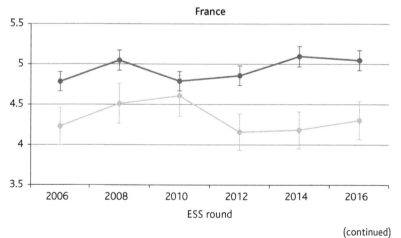

(continued)

Figure 8.7: Economic insecurity and attitudes towards a multicultural society – different countries (continued)

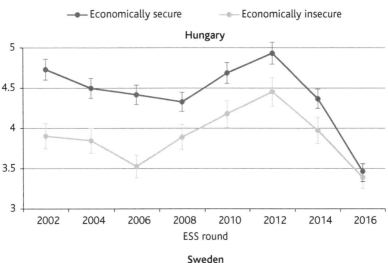

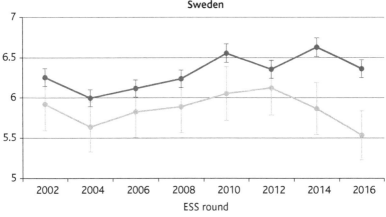

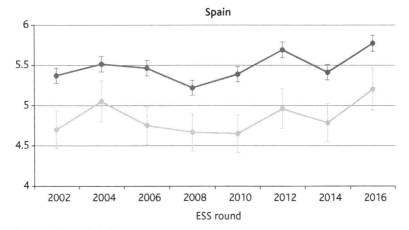

Source: ESS rounds 1–8

Conclusion

There are several central points that can be emphasised from the data analysed in this chapter. The first is that there is a general trend across different societal contexts that support for populist parties is rising. However, the magnitude and the level of influence that populist parties have vary across countries, which also indicates that the causality between a rise in support and national welfare policies is not necessarily simple. There is thus no evidence, except for Hungary, that rising support for populism reflects a broader hostility towards immigrants and a multicultural society. Positive attitudes towards immigrants and a multicultural society seem to be rather stable or slightly increasing. In Hungary, we see a rapid decline in support for a multicultural society. Despite the fact that general attitudes towards immigrants have not changed, we find an increase in support for less generous policies towards refugees.

Another point is that welfare chauvinism is most widespread in Hungary and least in Sweden, although data end in 2016 and later developments could have changed this. Attitudes towards immigrants' welfare rights in France, Spain and Germany might reflect the dual labour market structure, in which rights are earned through labour market participation, implying that citizens might be less worried about non-natives getting benefits that they have not contributed to. This is in contrast to universal welfare states that have more universal types of benefits, even when there are conditions for receiving them.

Finally, in France, Germany, the UK and Sweden, there seems to be a growing polarisation between the economically vulnerable and the economically secure segments of society with regard to attitudes towards immigrants, while in Hungary, we find a growing consensus between the economically secure and insecure on a negative view of immigration. Overall, together with the points from Chapter 7, this points to the fact that at least part of welfare chauvinism and the rise in support for populist parties go hand in hand.

Note

[1]   Figure from www.dr.dk (accessed 13 September 2018).

References

European Commission (2018) *Public opinion in the European Union.* Standard Eurobarometer 89, Spring, Brussels: European Commission.

Inglehart, R. and Norris, P. (2016) Trump, Brexit, and the rise of populism: economic have-nots and cultural backlash. HKS Faculty Research Working Paper, Harvard Kennedy School.

Lubbers, M., Gijsberts, M. and Scheepers, P (2002) Extreme right-wing voting in Western Europe. *European Journal of Political Research*, 41(3): 345–78.

Standing, G. (2011) *The precariat: The dangerous new class.* London: Bloomsbury Academic.

Concluding remarks

Introduction

This last chapter aims to sum up what can be considered central aspects and elements to be aware of if connecting populism, welfare chauvinism and developments in welfare states. First, though, in the second section, there is a discussion of whether there has been permanent austerity and/or retrenchment, including how and whether this can be seen in relation to those who are perceived as deserving compared to those seen as undeserving. In the third section, some of the most central lessons from the analysis are presented, whereas in the fourth section, the attempt is made to try to draw some policy conclusions, with reflections on how change in policies might have an impact on welfare state development. This also includes a few suggestions related to how welfare states can develop in the years to come. Lastly, in the fifth section, there is a final summary.

Retrenchment: seemingly not the only game in town?

As discussed, especially in Chapter 5, the data indicate that in many welfare states, there has not been de facto retrenchment or austerity with regard to overall levels of welfare spending since the financial crisis. This is not to say that there have not been any cuts in specific social policy areas, and, further, that it might have been felt as austerity by groups whose conditions have deteriorated due to tighter conditions for receiving, for example, welfare benefits. Even with real increases in overall spending, a higher number of people eligible for services as a consequence of demographic developments, such as in the field of elderly care, might also be experienced by individuals in need of services as austerity. Within the pension system, with a certain time lag, there might also be a relative reduction in replacement rates and increases in the eligible pension age for receiving old-age pensions, as well as the possibility that the replacement rate will be further reduced over time. Still, the data seem to indicate that within the pension field, there is still a better replacement rate for many low-income earners, although with variations across countries.

This possible, although very slow and gradual, reduction in pensions is in contrast to old people often being seen as those who deserve benefits and/or services. At the same time, the elderly have been a growing group of the electorate, and if pursuing self-interest (see Chapter 2), one should have expected that this development of a reduction in spending on pensions would not have taken place. A possible reason could be that the chosen implementation period for changes in the pension system has been very long in most countries, that the changes in the systems might be difficult to understand due to their complexities and also that there has been a stronger willingness to accept changes in times of economic crisis. This is further combined with the fact that the elderly not only live longer, but are also in generally better health than previous generations, and in many countries, they now stay longer in the labour market. This might have made changes more acceptable than one could have expected at the outset. Still, overall spending on old age has increased (see Chapter 5).

In some countries, however, there has also been a decline in the replacement rate related to unemployment benefit and social assistance after the financial crisis. Therefore, in combination with tighter conditions for eligibility in some countries, this can be seen as a reason for the fact that some people have perceived the development as one of retrenchment.

There are differences among countries but, overall, there is seemingly still more money available in real terms at the macro-level for welfare policies. This does not indicate that there are not welfare services where there has been implicit austerity because more people will need services for almost the same amount of money, for example, due to more people being in need. Neither does it show that welfare states are not under pressure, and that the rise of more populist approaches in several areas, despite right-wing national chauvinism often being behind it, is something that has only to a limited extent reduced welfare state development in spending on welfare. In particular, welfare services seem to have increased, whereas certain benefits have been reduced. An implicit paternalistic issue might also prevail in the sense that when it comes to the delivery of welfare services, all can see where the spending goes to, whereas income transfers can be spent as the individual prefers. For some, this is compared to the income one receives when working in the labour market (see Chapter 6). Seen in this light, neoliberal ideas of the need for reductions in the public sector have not been pursued in all countries.

At the same time, in several European Union (EU) countries, there has been an expansion of expenditures within the fields of old age, sickness/health and day care for children. However, the picture is blurred as spending in million euros per inhabitant in fixed prices has increased, while there has been a reduction in the replacement rate for the unemployed and in pensions. It is therefore obvious that retrenchment in welfare state development has not been the only game in town. Still, it fits with the fact that there is support for services to those seen as deserving and native, which in most countries, is still the case in relation to welfare services.

What have we learnt?

Central for the populist stance and voters' support thereof seems to be that a 'them and us' understanding can be established, and that it is possible to find at least one group or concept (such as migrants, free movement and/or globalisation) that can be seen as, and be given the role of, scapegoat. It also points to the fact that what might be beneficial at the societal level can still have winners and losers at the micro-level. In line with a self-interest argument, those who gain, for example, from globalisation and the free movement of workers will also be in favour of the changes arising from the impact thereof as they might benefit by higher wages and lower prices on certain private goods. However, the same need not be the case for those who have lost their job and/or witnessed a decline in their real wage level as a consequence of the global development and standard of living. They will, most likely, be against these changes, even though this perception might be mediated by the impact of the welfare state and/or that their children/grandchildren gain from it.

The increasing social, political and economic rights of groups who, for various reasons (ethnicity, gender, sexual preferences, migrants), have been given better positions and entitlements in society might, at the same time, be seen by some as others getting something while their own position in society is no longer the same. Therefore, it may be seen as promoting the position of others at their expense. Thus, the improved situation for groups previously having weaker positions can open the way for other groups in society to blame this for negative changes in their options and standard of living, and a feeling of being pushed to the back of the queue by these groups.

Part of the explanation can therefore also be that we have seen a growing divide in societies. Inequality has been on the rise not only in terms of economic inequality, but also in other parts of societies' development, such as education, health, influence and so on. Rising inequality and stagnant real wages can be an argument for some people that there is a need to change policy direction. A paradox here is that rising inequality is especially related to changes in tax and spending policies, and right-wing parties are often in favour of reducing taxes. Stagnant real wages can have a variety of reasons, including structural changes in societies as a consequence of new technology and globalisation; however, naturally, it can also be a response to a more open labour market and increased migration in some sectors. In these cases, it seems that migrants are often used as scapegoats, despite the fact that this may not be the reason for the change, and that there could even have been a lack of manpower in some countries without the influx of migrant workers.

The structural transformation of societies, which is likely to be even stronger in the years to come than that witnessed before, can imply that groups who cannot get a job might see their hopes of having a better life dwindling away, not only for themselves, but also for their children. Given the centrality of having a job in many countries in order to feel included and have consumption opportunities, in such circumstances where hope is reduced, this can easily lead to a conflict, with an understanding of the fact that some are taking away their good position in society. For example, this is often illustrated by arguing that migrants are to be blamed for the development, with a more welfare chauvinistic approach in welfare state policies as a response. Growing levels of unemployment and economic insecurity (due to the declining replacement rate) can also therefore be seen as a reason for support for populism and welfare chauvinism because (as argued in Chapter 3) losing one's job has a strong negative impact on well-being and happiness. Structural changes in societies, even if benefitting overall development, also need to be interpreted in relation to the consequences of the change for the worst off in a Rawlsian understanding.

There still seems to be a high level of support in most countries for having a welfare state, despite the changes that have taken place. This is also despite the fact that general trust in governments has been on the decline. A contradiction against self-interest as a reason for the development in the legitimacy of welfare states is that in most welfare states from 2008 to 2016, there has been an increase in support for childcare services for working parents being the responsibility of the state. At the same time, there has been reduced support for a reasonable standard of living for the elderly being the government's responsibility, and in most countries, less surprisingly, there has been more of a decline than an increase with regard to a reasonable standard of living for the unemployed being the responsibility of the government. Part of these developments reflects differences in historical trajectories in various welfare states and what citizens expect from their welfare state, but also that self-interest alone is not able to explain changes in attitudes to welfare states. However, it also reflects that the replacement rate has been lowered for the unemployed, which will also happen in the future for pensioners. Thus, despite welfare chauvinism and populism, which would be expected to go against a reduction for pensioners, the electorate seems to have accepted these changes in the years after the financial crisis, while also accepting higher spending on day care for children.

Some policy conclusions

There seem to be some central, but important, policy conclusions deriving from the analysis and data presented in this book. The first is that it is important to create jobs and help people to be able to earn their own income and have something to get up for in the morning, as witnessed by the strong decline in trust in government after the financial crisis. Jobs can support social cohesion, and also presumably reduce mistrust in the government and policymakers. This is because having a job is central for those of working age and very important for their well-being. In a way, this goes back to the central message of the Clinton campaign in 1992: 'It's the Economy Stupid'.[1] Using economic policy to create jobs – not only by arguing for a work-first approach or a blind belief in economic incentives by reducing the level of benefits, but also through strong investment-led economic growth (both public and private) – would cause overall better living conditions, but presumably also higher support for the welfare state and more socially cohesive societies. In times of economic growth, it is easier to accept growing spending on welfare policies as this can often be done without having to increase the level of taxes and duties as the money can be found from the growth in the revenue from taxes and duties arising from the automatic stabilisers in the fiscal system. Investment, understood in a broad context, also includes social investment in education and good childcare, not only infrastructure and support for the development of private companies. Even small increases in taxes and duties would presumably be possible in times of economic growth as this would not be in contradiction with a growth in private consumption as well.

How to create jobs is another matter, and it will be a problem globally if a tendency to protect jobs in individual countries is followed as this will reduce global trade. Compensation to those losing out from international and technological development can be an important aspect in getting people to accept the growing impact of globalisation on national and international development.

The other issue that it is important to deal with is to reduce the level of inequality in most countries given the often strong increase in economic inequality witnessed in recent years, with its negative impact not only on economic growth, but also on social capital. It is well known that there does not seem to be a documented impact of a trickle-down economic policy whereby economic growth will make all people better off, and given that high levels of inequality (as shown in Chapter 3) influence many other spheres of society, policies that reduce inequality might have a positive impact on social cohesion and reduce mistrust towards decision-makers. This may thereby also reduce support for the extreme parts of populist parties. Reducing inequality will also cause a change of resources towards groups with a higher tendency to spend, and thereby increase overall economic demand for goods and services in itself, as well as the ability to keep or create jobs.

Migration and the free movement of workers can still be important aspects of both regional and global development. Here, it seems to be important that this takes place in an orderly way and not in such a way that it pushes wages down through a variety of social dumping developments. In order to avoid pressure on the ability to finance welfare spending, some international agreements on a stronger fight against tax havens could also reduce support for populism, and in order to finance welfare states, agreements on a minimum corporate income tax could also be highly important. Thereby, in a global world, there are still, and presumably to a greater extent than ever, important areas to collaborate about internationally. This may also help in reducing the perception that global and regional economic development is only beneficial for the rich, companies and insiders in the labour market, rather than in a broader sense for all in society. The conflict between what might be good at societal and global levels, and everyday experience in local neighbourhoods, needs carefully designed interventions to ensure that all parts of society gain and can feel the gain from regional and global economic development.

Conclusion

There has been a rise in the number of countries with an increase in support for a more populist stance towards welfare state development. There has been a discrediting of those not seen as deserving, frequently migrants and refugees. Economic development after the financial crisis has been varied and economic inequality has been on the rise in most countries.

Destabilising elements have been strong in many countries, and a strong turn towards nationalism and welfare chauvinism has been part of the development, with a few exceptions dependent on national circumstances. Countries harder hit by the financial crisis seem to have stronger support for more populist parties and politics – in line with the fact that jobs and trust in the future can have a role for people's perception of how they would like to see the development in the country that they are living in. Therefore, the development and attitudes towards having a more nativist strategy of welfare state development is not that surprising, although it might be in conflict with the historical understanding that support to the middle class is an important aspect of how welfare states develop as this helps in ensuring a majority in favour of the welfare state.

The populist often supports more right-wing parties, again with a few exceptions, and therefore leans towards a more neoliberal economic policy in principle. However, at the same time, this has not implied strong and persistent austerity when looking into the development of welfare state spending overall. In most of the countries included in the analysis here, there has been an overall positive development in welfare state spending, including when trying to take inflation and demographic issues into consideration (see the details in Chapter 5). At the same time, there has been retrenchment in relation to certain welfare benefits, especially related to unemployment, but also with regard to pensions in some countries. In particular, development in benefits to the unemployed and those outside the labour market can seemingly be explained by an often negative stance towards migrants and the non-native unemployed, while, at the same time, also hitting natives who become unemployed.

However, the in-depth stories depicted in Chapter 6 clearly indicate that the perception of who should and should not have support is deeply embedded in an understanding of how societies have been functioning and what the causes are for the development. This was further followed up in Chapters 7 and 8 with an analysis of attitudes towards different parts of welfare state development and immigrants.

The development of more spending on welfare, especially in service areas including health care, can be argued to follow a line where this is understood as being to those who are deserving. Therefore, those parties wanting to gain power, even if they would like to reduce the welfare state in principle, are also willing and prepared to spend more as this is supported by electoral groups who demand strong support for parts of welfare state spending and, at the same time, negative policies towards migrants. This helps in explaining the paradox of populist development with right-wing arguments, where despite stronger support for the private sector, they are not able to limit welfare state development overall.

The rise of populism also implies more diverse societies, which could cause less social cohesion in the years to come; thereby, it cannot be taken for granted that there will not be a future backlash to welfare state development. Overall, this points to the fact that policies that create jobs, reduce inequality and help in the social integration of societies will, presumably, be the best guarantee for stable societal developments. There is therefore still a need for strong welfare states.

Note

[1] See, for example, www.huffingtonpost.com/jerry-jasinowski/presidential-debates_b_8478456.html (accessed 15 January 2018).

Index

References to tables and figures are in *italics*.